D1258768

Hardy Orchids

Hardy Orchids

Orchids for the garden and frost-free glasshouse

PHILLIP CRIBB &
CHRISTOPHER BAILES

CHRISTOPHER HELM
London

TIMBER PRESS
Portland, Oregon

©1989 Phillip Cribb and Christopher Bailes
Line illustrations by Cherry-Anne Lavish and Valerie Price

Christopher Helm (Publishers) Ltd, Imperial House, 21-25 North Street,
Bromley, Kent BR1 1SD

ISBN 0-7470-0416-1

A CIP catalogue record for this book is available from the British Library.

All rights reserved. No reproduction, copy or transmission of this publication may be made without written permission.

No paragraph of this publication may be reproduced, copied or transmitted
save with written permission or in accordance with the provisions of the
Copyright Act 1956 (as amended), or under the terms of any licence
permitting limited copying issued by the Copyright Licensing Agency,
7 Ridgmount Street, London WC1E 7AE.

Any person who does any unauthorised act in relation to this publication
may be liable to criminal prosecution and civil claims for damages.

First published in North America
in 1989 by
Timber Press, Inc.
9999 SW Wilshire
Portland, Oregon 97225
USA

ISBN 0-88192-147-5

THE HOLDEN ARBORETUM
LIBRARY

Typeset by Leaper & Gard
Printed and bound in Great Britain by Butler and Tanner,
Frome, Somerset

6632

Contents

Colour Plates

Cymbidium goeringii

Figures

Acknowledgements

Many friends have helped us in the preparation of this book and have given freely of their time and experience. We would like to thank Maurice and Margaret Mason, Alan Bloom, Dr Tom Norman, Lady Lisa Sainsbury, Christopher Grey-Wilson, Brian Mathew, David Menzies, Mark Clements, Joyce Stewart, Jeffrey Wood, Brian Halliwell, Stephanie Joseph, Tony Hall, Paddy Woods, Gerry Munday, Soo Tasker, Ian Butterfield, Robert Mitchell, Sandra Bell, Samuel Sprunger, Dr Jany Renz, Dora Gerhard, Dr Adelaide Stork, Dr Klaus Amman, Dr Ernst Grell, Helen Richards and many others for their help and encouragement. Much of our experience of the cultivation of these orchids has been gained at the Royal Botanic Gardens at Kew and we would like to thank the Director, Keeper and Curator for letting us use the facilities there.

We appreciate very much the use of photographs by Dora Gerhard, David Menzies, Paul Davies, Maryse Kolakowski, Bruno Erny, Dr Carl Luer, Ed Greenwood, J. Delamain, Sandra Bell, Robert Mitchell, Isobyl and Eric La Croix, David Chesterman, Derek Turner Ettlinger, R. Zabeau, M. Svanderlik and A. McRobb.

We would also like to thank our wives Marianne and Helen for their support whilst this book was being written.

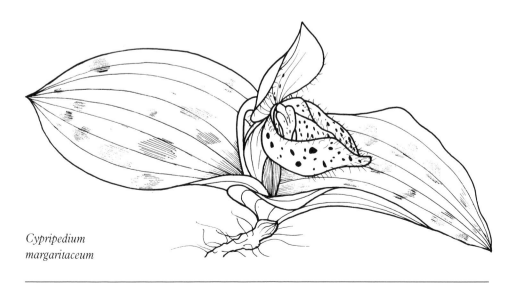

Cypripedium
margaritaceum

Introduction

Orchids have never featured to any great extent as garden plants in the temperate regions of the world despite the undoubted popularity of the tropical species as subjects for the heated glasshouse. This is perhaps scarcely surprising when it is remembered that the temperate regions have relatively few species of orchids while the vast majority of orchids are to be found in the tropics and subtropics. Most of these species do not care for the low temperatures of the winter months and will generally not survive frosting. And yet, in this large and diverse family, there are still many species that will survive quite happily in a temperate environment and can be supposed to be hardy even in inclement climates, such as those of western and northern Europe and North America. Furthermore, it is a mistake to suppose that the tropical and subtropical species all need hot and steamy conditions to survive. Many of these grow in mountainous regions where the temperature can at times drop to freezing or below. Some of these orchids exhibit a degree of hardiness and can be coaxed to grow with a minimum of protection in temperate areas.

We hope to show that the range of orchids that can be grown out of doors in temperate climes is much greater than most gardeners appreciate. Using the British Isles as a basis, we have included here all of the orchids that are truly hardy throughout most of the country and those that will survive outside in the milder south west but will need a degree of protection elsewhere. The corresponding climatic zones in North America are zones 2 to 7 (Rehder, 1940). Most of the half-hardy orchids will grow happily in the Alpine glasshouse where temperatures are kept above freezing in the winter months. To this extent the orchids dis-

cussed in this book can be considered as Alpines and are, in the British Isles, most commonly seen in the gardens and collections of alpine plant growers and nurseries. The Royal Horticultural Society has followed this prevailing philosophy by sending hardy and half-hardy orchids to its Rock Garden Committee for judging while all of the other orchids, mostly tropical epiphytes and their hybrids, are sent to the Orchid Committee.

Orchids have fascinated generations of gardeners and the irregularity of their appearance in the garden cannot be explained by any lack of interest. As early as 1597 John Gerard, the herbalist, was growing in his garden the Lady's Slipper Orchid, a plant he had received from his friend Mr Garrett, an apothecary. Hardy orchids, such as *Cypripedium*, *Orchis* and *Ophrys* species also appear in the early volumes of *Curtis's Botanical Magazine* in the early years of the 19th century but it is safe to suggest that most of these orchids made only fleeting appearances in cultivation, dying out after flowering once or twice to delight their owners. The truth seems to be that most orchids, even the hardy ones, require particular conditions to enable them to thrive. A few, such as the marsh orchids, are relatively tolerant of a range of conditions and will survive many years in gardens, but the majority seem to need special care. Species, such as the temperate slipper orchids, with a reputation for being difficult to grow, do sometimes thrive and flower spectacularly well in gardens. This suggests that an observant gardener can succeed with these orchids. In our experience, those likely to succeed with the hardy species are those who have taken the trouble to study the biology and especially the ecological requirements of their orchids.

The discovery in the early years of the present century that revolutionised our approach to orchid culture was that all orchids can only germinate in the presence of a mycorrhizal fungus. The relationship is a particularly intimate one that can survive throughout the lifetime of many species. We suggest here that growers adopt an ecological approach to the cultivation of hardy orchids, appreciating the intimate mycorrhizal association which seems to be particularly important for the terrestrial orchids. This approach has produced spectacular results in the pot cultivation of European orchids at Kew, including many species that had previously been considered a waste of the gardener's time. Plants that previously survived for only a year or two before dying out have grown vigorously under the adopted regime, have multiplied and flowered freely. Attention to the requirements of both the orchid and its fungal partner has underpinned this programme and the results to date have more than justified this approach.

The literature on hardy and half-hardy orchids is not very large when compared to the flood of publications on their exotic relatives. For over fifty years the standard text on the subject has been A.W. Darnell's *Orchids for the Outdoor Garden* published in 1930. Sadly, of the many hundreds of orchids described there, only a small percentage are truly hardy or even suitable for the alpine house. Darnell's book is a catalogue of species from the world's temperate regions and from the higher mountains of the tropics and sub-tropics. Many of these have never been introduced into cultivation, and more that have did not survive long. The cold tolerance of these orchids is not in question but the ability of many to survive the temperate winter's combination of damp and cold is less certain.

The only other extensive account of hardy orchids that we know is in the second volume of C.H. Grey's comprehensive *Hardy Bulbs* published in 1938. This, however, acknowledges Darnell's work as its major source. Short treatments of hardy orchids are to be found in many of the books on Alpine plants, notably those of Reginald Farrer and Royton Heath. The pages of the specialist orchid and alpine plant journals are also worth consulting and we recommend the excellent quarterly *Bulletin of the Alpine Garden Society*, the Royal Horticultural Society's monthly magazine, *The Garden*, and the specialist orchid journals, such as the *Orchid Review*, *Die Orchidee* and *The American Orchid Society Bulletin*, for their frequent articles on temperate orchids in cultivation and in their native habitats.

We, therefore, make no apology for producing this account of a group of plants that we feel have been unjustly neglected in the past or, if not neglected, then badly mistreated.

The Structure of Orchids

No one really knows how many species of orchids there are in the world, but the family is certainly extraordinarily diverse, with estimates ranging from 15,000 to 30,000 species. Although the family is at its most successful and diverse in the tropics and subtropics, orchids are found beyond the Arctic Circle in the north and as far south as Macquarie Island, which lies between Australia and the Antarctic. The diversity of form found in this wide-ranging group is therefore scarcely surprising. The smallest orchids, such as the aptly named Australian *Bulbophyllum minutissimum*, measure no more than a few millimetres across, while the liana-like *Vanilla imperialis* from Central and East Africa will climb into the tops of rain forest trees.

The flower

The distinctive features of orchids which separate them from other flowering plants lie in their flowers. These are simple in structure and yet highly modified from the more typical monocotyledon flower, as exemplified by *Trillium* or *Lilium*, to which orchids are very distantly allied. These characteristically have their floral parts arranged in threes or multiples of three. Orchids are no exception and this can most easily be seen in the two other whorls of the flower. The floral parts are situated at the apex of the ovary which itself can be seen to be tripartite in many orchids. The lowest whorl of the flower is the calyx which, in

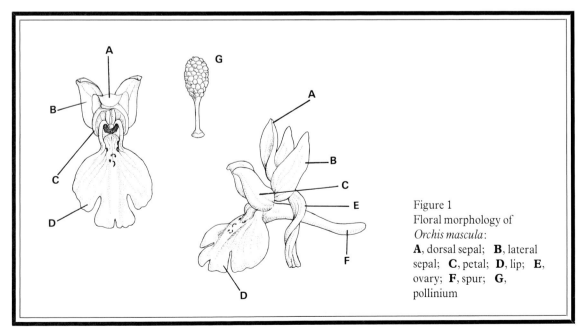

Figure 1
Floral morphology of *Orchis mascula*:
A, dorsal sepal; **B**, lateral sepal; **C**, petal; **D**, lip; **E**, ovary; **F**, spur; **G**, pollinium

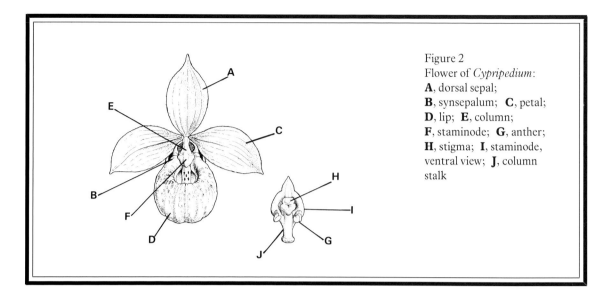

Figure 2
Flower of *Cypripedium*:
A, dorsal sepal;
B, synsepalum; **C**, petal;
D, lip; **E**, column;
F, staminode; **G**, anther;
H, stigma; **I**, staminode,
ventral view; **J**, column
stalk

orchids, consists of three sepals which may be green or more or less brightly coloured and even petaloid. Often the two lateral sepals differ from the third, called the dorsal, to varying degrees. In most of the slipper orchids, for example, they are united to form a synsepalum.

The corolla also comprises three petals which are usually brightly coloured. The two lateral petals are, in most species, uppermost in the flower and differ markedly from the third petal, which lies at the bottom of the flower. The third petal, called the lip or labellum, is often highly modified, lobed or tripartite. The upper surface is adorned with a callus of raised ridges, lamellae or tufts, or areas of hairs or glands. In many species the lip is extended at the base to form a saccate to filiform spur which may or may not contain nectar. The lip is an important adaptation of the orchid to facilitate cross pollination. It can be imagined as a brightly coloured flag to attract potential and specific pollinators, which are then guided towards the pollen and stigmatic surface by the form of the callus. The lip, therefore, can be supposed to act as a landing platform and the callus structure as a guidance system for the pollinator.

The central part of the orchid flower shows the greatest modifications to the basic monocotyledon pattern. Reduction in the number of floral parts and fusion of the male and female organs into a single structure have been the major evolutionary

forces at work. The fused organ in the centre of the orchid flower is called the column. In most orchids a single anther lies at the apex of the column. The anther does not contain powdery pollen, as in most plants; the pollen is borne in a number of discrete masses, called pollinia, of which there are usually two, four or rarely eight. In the slipper orchids, there are two anthers on the column, placed on each side behind the large shield-shaped sterile anther, the staminode. Another primitive group, the tropical Asiatic Apostasioideae, comprising the two genera *Apostasia* and *Neuwiedia*, also have two or even three anthers.

The stigma is also positioned on the column of the orchid, usually on the ventral surface. The stigma is usually a lobed sticky depression situated below and behind the anther; but in some terrestrial genera, such as *Habenaria*, the stigma is bilobed with the receptive surfaces at the apex of each lobe. In many species the pollen masses are transferred to the stigmatic surface by a modified lobe of the stigma called the rostellum. This is developed as a projection of various shapes that catches the pollen masses as the pollinator passes beneath on its way out of the flower.

An interesting feature of the development of most orchid flowers is the phenomenon of resupination. In bud, the lip lies uppermost in the flower while the column lies lowermost. In species with a pendent inflorescence the lip will, therefore, naturally lie lowermost in the flower when it opens. However, this would not be the case in the many species with erect infloresences. Here the opening of the flower would naturally lead to the lip assuming a place at the top of the flower above the column. This is the situation in the rare European Ghost Orchid, *Epipogium aphyllum*. In most species this is not the case and the lip is lowermost in the flower. This position is achieved by means of a twisting of the flower stalk or ovary through 180° as the bud develops. This twisting is termed resupination.

The vegetative morphology

The vegetative features of orchids are, if anything, more variable than their floral ones. This is scarcely surprising, given the variety of habitats in which orchids are found. Orchids grow in almost every situation: the steamy year-long heat of the tropical rain forest; the dramatic seasonality of the Arctic tundra; and the arid margins of the deserts of Arabia. The major adaptations seen in orchid vegetative morphology have evolved to combat adverse environmental conditions; in particular, the problems of water conservation and marked seasonality.

That tropical orchids might suffer from periodic water deficits is not immediately obvious. Rainfall is not continuous even in the wettest habitats and in many places even in the tropics the rainfall patterns are markedly seasonal. Furthermore, most tropical orchids are epiphytic, growing on the trunks, branches and twigs of trees. In this situation, water run-off is rapid and the orchids will dry rapidly in the sunshine that follows the rain. Many orchids have therefore developed marked adaptations of one or more organs to allow them to survive these periodic droughts. Some of these adaptations are as dramatic as those encountered in the Cactaceae. The stem can develop into a water storage organ, and this is so common in tropical orchids that the resulting structure is called a pseudobulb. In *Bulbophyllum* species the pseudobulb is of one node only while in *Dendrobium* and *Eria* it comprises several nodes. Pseudobulbs are also found in many terrestrial

orchids and can grow either above the ground, as in *Calanthe*, or underground, as in many *Eulophia* species.

The leaf is another organ that has undergone dramatic modification in the orchids. Fleshy or leathery leaves with restricted stomata are common. The leaves of species growing in the drier places can be terete, as in the tropical Asiatic *Luisia* and *Papilionanthe*, while in genera such as *Taeniophyllum* and *Microcoelia*, the leaves have been reduced to scales and their photosynthetic function taken over by flattened green roots.

The roots themselves are much modified in most epiphytic orchids, being adapted for two functions: attachment to the substrate, and water and nutrient uptake in a periodically dry environment. The roots have an active growing tip but, behind this, the root is covered by an envelope of dead empty cells called a velamen. This protects the inner conductive tissue of the roots and may also aid the uptake of moisture from the atmosphere, acting almost as blotting paper for the orchid.

As can be seen life in the tropics can be inhospitable even for orchids. In those regions with a more marked seasonality, conditions may be positively hostile for orchids at certain times of the year. Even tropical forests and woods can have periods of relative drought where the orchids have to survive days or even weeks without rain falling. In these conditions, tropical orchids without water-storage capabilities in their stems or leaves can drop their leaves and survive on the moisture stored in their roots, which are protected by their cover of velamen.

In temperate regions of the world, orchids may similarly need to survive an extensive dry period; for example, in the Mediterranean region of Europe. The summer months there are the dry ones and the orchids, which are all terrestrial, survive as tuberoids (usually incorrectly called tubers) or swollen roots growing through the wetter winter months. In northern Europe and in North America, the winter weather is too severe for the orchids to grow through the winter when temperatures well below freezing may be common. The orchids then survive the winter in a dormant state as tuberoids, swollen roots or rhi-

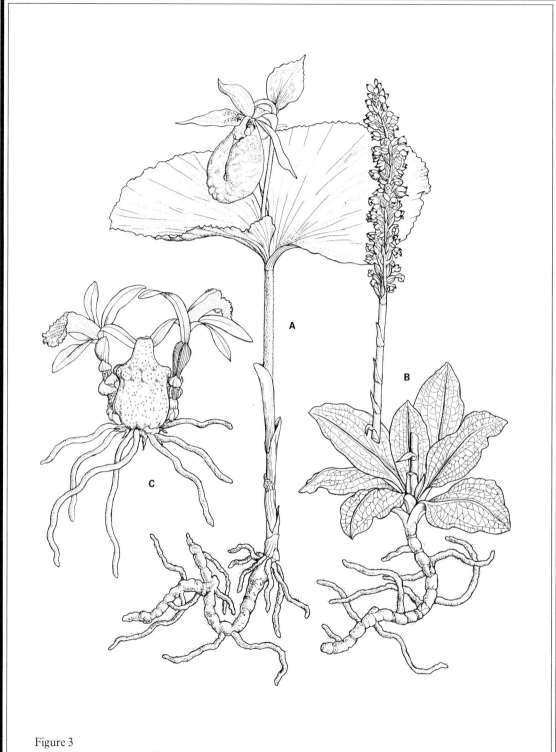

Figure 3
Vegetative morphology of rhizomatous and pseudobulbous orchids: **A**, *Cypripedium*; **B**, *Goodyera*; **C**, *Pleione*

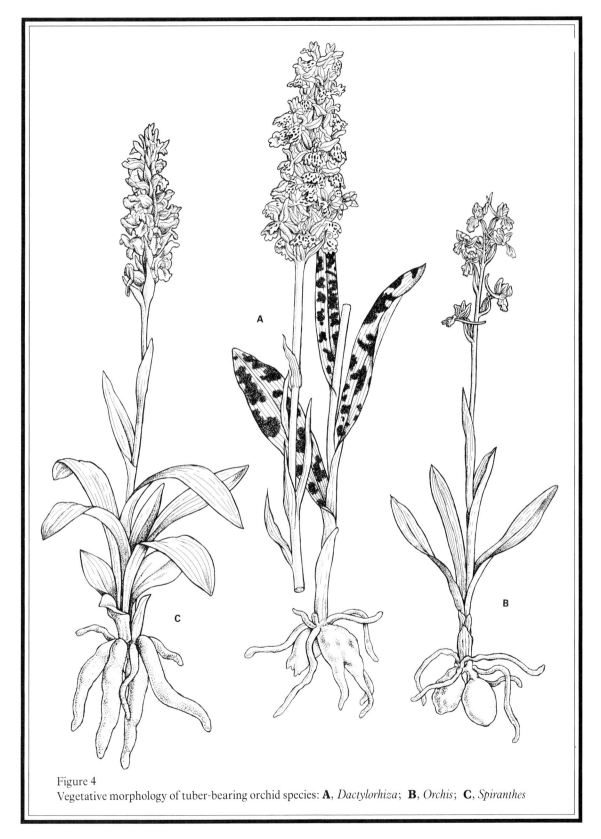

Figure 4
Vegetative morphology of tuber-bearing orchid species: **A**, *Dactylorhiza*; **B**, *Orchis*; **C**, *Spiranthes*

zomes. Growth commences in the spring and continues through the summer months.

An appreciation of the appropriate growing season, and how each species survives through its dormant season, are therefore of considerable importance to growers of hardy and near hardy orchids. These are usually species from the temperate areas of the world or from the high mountains of the tropics and subtropics. All of these have a dormant period induced by either drought or cold, often a combination of the two. In the British Isles, more orchids are lost in the dormancy of winter months than at any other time and this is often due to the prevalence of damp winter conditions. Many orchids will survive periods of low temperature if kept dry but will rapidly perish if the same tubers are kept moist.

The Life History of Orchids

An understanding of the extraordinary natural history of orchids will assist anyone considering cultivating this fascinating group of plants. It is perhaps commonplace to say that all life on Earth is interdependent but, with orchids, this aphorism is particularly well illustrated. The life cycle of an orchid depends upon its relationship with a particular fungus and also, in most cases, with a particular pollinating animal, usually an insect.

Our knowledge of the role of the fungus in the life cycle of an orchid was discovered in the early years of this century by the French scientist, Noel Bernard, and elucidated by the German, Hans Burgeff. Only in recent years has their pioneering work been continued, most notably by the Australian botanists, Jack Warcup (1985) and Mark Clements (1988). Orchids produce seed that is dust-like and amongst the smallest of all flowering plants. The seed comprises a seed coat or testa which encloses the embryo of 100-200 cells. Orchid seeds contains no endosperm, the food store that comprises the bulk of most other seeds. Therefore, the orchid seed has no integral food store to enable the seed to germinate and grow on

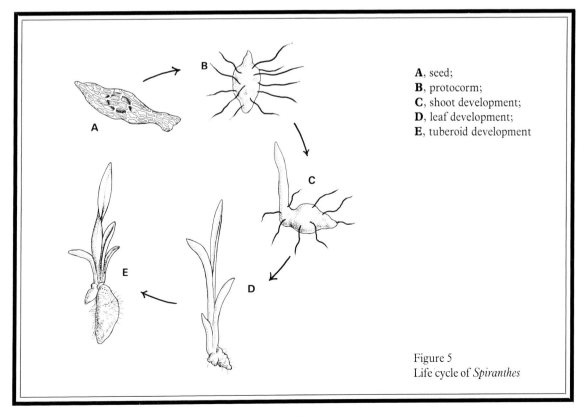

A, seed;
B, protocorm;
C, shoot development;
D, leaf development;
E, tuberoid development

Figure 5
Life cycle of *Spiranthes*

its own, given the right environmental conditions. This potentially disastrous state of affairs has been overcome by the development of an intimate symbiosis between the orchid and an appropriate fungus, which is called a mycorrhiza, present in some soils.

In appropriate conditions, a mycorrhizal hypha will penetrate one end of the orchid embryo through its large suspensor cell. As the fungus enters the inner cells of the embryo, the orchid begins to digest the fungal hyphae thereby releasing nutrients to fuel the growth of the orchid. The germinating orchid develops into a small elongate top-shaped or spindle-shaped body called a protocorm. The protocorm continues to grow until the first seedling leaf and roots are produced. The balance between fungal penetration and digestion is critical until the orchid has produced green chlorophyll-bearing leaves, when the dependency upon the fungal partner declines and may even cease. In most tropical epiphytic species the role of the mycorrhizal fungus appears to be confined to the early stages of the development of the orchid. However, there is strong empirical evidence to suggest that in temperate terrestrial species the symbiotic relationship may be important throughout the life of an orchid. The European Bird's Nest Orchid, *Neottia nidus-avis*, and the Ghost Orchid, *Epipogium aphyllum*, for example, never produce leaves and only appear above the ground to flower. Their entire development depends upon the ability of their mycorrhizae to provide them with nutrients, a testimony to the potential of this bizarre relationship.

This observation has considerable consequences for the grower. It could explain why European terrestrial orchids often die out quickly in cultivation. Either the mycorrhizal fungus was not transferred with the orchid or, even more probably, the fungus did not care for the environment into which it had been brought and consequently died. The death of the orchid usually follows soon afterwards. It may be that the grower should attend more to the conditions that suit the fungus than to those that apparently suit the orchid.

We still have a great deal to discover about the relationships of orchids and their mycorrhizal fungi. The specificity of the relationship is still debated, although recent work has indicated at least some degree of specificity in the European and Australian terrestrial species. One of the main problems is our poor knowledge of the taxonomy of the fungi involved. Fungi that look alike do not necessarily produce germination in the same batch of orchid seed. A second area that needs further study is that illustrated by Clements (1987) when he suggested that the fungi may be symbionts of other plants at the same time as their relationship with an orchid. The observation that the two species of the Australian underground orchid, *Rhizanthella*, are always associated with *Melaleuca* bushes it strongly suggestive that this may sometimes be the case.

At the other end of the life cycle, orchids are also dependent upon rather specific relationships for their successful reproduction. Orchids have unusual flowers, some species fancifully resembling bees, wasps, flies, spiders, monkeys and dancing ladies. However, a serious purpose lurks behind this charming menagerie. The orchid flowers are designed to attract pollinators that will ensure fertilisation and seed production for the continuation of the species. The deception is most elaborate in the genus *Ophrys* where the flowers of most species resemble bees or wasps. This resemblance is far from accidental and fools not only us but also those very insects that are mimicked. The flowers emit a scent that is a powerful attractant to males of species of solitary bees. The shape and patterns of the lip of the flower resembles those on the body of the female bee providing an additional stimulus to the male; the hairs on the lip also resemble those on the female bee. On alighting on the lip, the male, in attempting to mate with the flower, is brought into contact with the pollinia at the apex of the column. These stick to the body of the bee and are removed when it leaves the flower. Cross pollination is ensured when the bee visits another flower and repeats its abortive attempt to mate there.

Most other orchids are cross pollinated by attracting insects by a variety of means, in some tropical orchids even more bizarre than that of *Ophrys*. Pollination mechanisms are usually relatively species-specific although hybridisation is not infrequent in the wild in some groups of orchids. The genus *Dactylorhiza* is noted for its propensity to hybridise in Europe and it has proved a nightmare for the botanist hoping to classify the species.

Some orchids have eliminated the hit-and-miss chanciness of cross pollination for the short-term safety of self pollination. The best-known example in Europe is the Bee Orchid, *Ophrys apifera*, which throughout most of its range is self pollinating. Several species of *Epipactis* have adopted a similar strategy with the pollen masses falling into the stigmatic cavity because of the absence of a rostellum.

Whatever the strategy adopted by orchids, successful pollination and fertilisation leads to the production of large numbers of seeds. A single seed pod of most European orchids will produce hundreds of dust-like seeds, while the tropical species usually produce even greater quantities. The Swan Orchid, *Cycnoches chlorochilon*, has been estimated, for example, to produce 3.75 million seeds in a single pod. The high seed production is achieved by the orchid seed's lack of an embryo. Fortunately, most of the mycorrhizal fungi seem to be widespread species and the production of large numbers of orchid seeds ensures that at least some will meet an appropriate fungus.

Our message to growers, therefore, is to take care of the mycorrhizal fungi — and the orchids will usually look after themselves.

The Ecology of Orchids

Orchids grow in a wide variety of habitats, from the rain forests of the tropics to the Arctic tundra. Hardy species considered here are mainly those of the temperate zones of the world and also a number of species from the higher mountains of the subtropics. An understanding of the way in which orchids grow in the wild is, in our opinion, the secret of their successful cultivation. Most orchids grow in rather precisely defined habitats, and we have already suggested that the morphological adaptations seen in an orchid's stem, roots and leaves are a reflection of the environment in which they grow.

Orchids as a family are a successful group both in terms of numbers of species and in the variety of habitats they have colonised. They have been particularly successful in the tropics and subtropics, where in places they can even form the dominant vegetation, as does *Phragmipedium caudatum* on some old lava flows in the Andes of Ecuador. The environment in which orchids have been most successful is the epiphytic one, where there is little competition from other flowering plants. In tropical Asia and Africa, we have seen as many as 20 or more species on the branches and trunk of a single tree. The ground orchids in these regions are seldom as prolific. Epiphytic species decline in numbers outside the tropics and few reach the temperate regions of the world. Indeed, none is to be found among Europe's 150 or so species, all of which are ground orchids.

The colder climates and seasonality of the temperate regions are the main reasons for their lack of epiphytes. We outline here a few of the environmental factors that might affect the growth of hardy and half-hardy orchids. More detailed ecological information can be found in the species' accounts in the Catalogue.

Climatic considerations

The yearly cycle of nearly all of the orchids considered here can be divided into an active growing season and a season of more or less marked dormancy. Active growth usually occurs when the weather is moist and mild. In Mediterranean climates, the active phase is from late autumn when the rains start through the winter until early spring. Leaf growth and the build-up of storage reserves in the roots or new tubers is usually completed by the time the flowering spike develops in the spring. Seed setting completes the cycle by late spring or early summer and the orchid enters a summer, dry-season dormant period. Many *Ophrys* species follow this cycle. Farther north and at higher elevations, the severe winter weather with frequent frost precludes growth during the winter. Vegetative growth will then start in the milder spring weather, with flowering occurring in late spring and summer, and the seed being shed in the late summer or autumn as the orchid enters its cold-induced dormancy. *Cypripedium* species follow this pattern in Europe and temperate North America.

Soil and substrate conditions

Nearly all of the orchids considered in this book have rather narrow substrate preferences in the wild. They are sensitive to soil pH, soil chemistry and soil structure. It seems likely, however, that the narrow substrate tolerances of orchids may reflect the specificity of their fungal symbiont more than that of the orchid itself.

Most of the European orchids grow in calcareous soils on chalk, limestone and calcareous sand or in calcareous fens and marshes. The pH of these soils is alkaline and high in calcium ions. In contrast, most Australian orchids prefer acidic nutrient-poor soils and will die rapidly in soils in which the European species thrive.

Few orchids grow in waterlogged conditions. Most prefer free-draining situations. A few species, such as the Fen Orchid, *Liparis loeselii*, and the North American *Spiranthes cernua* grow with their feet in water, but usually the roots or pseudobulbs of orchids growing in boggy or marginal areas are clear of the zone of permanent saturation.

Thus the provision of good drainage, and care in watering of hardy orchids, are critical to their cultivation, and must follow the natural seasonality of the plant.

Competition

In the wild, most terrestrial orchids are intolerant of the competition of other plants, particularly those with a rank growth. This is especially true in the early stages of development. In calcareous grassland, mature plants will survive in a closed turf but will not regenerate so readily, if at all. For this they require bare patches of soil relatively free of grass and other herbs. The weedy habit of some species of orchid is well known. The Bee Orchid, for example, is often a primary coloniser of bare soil on spoil heaps and roadsides but will eventually die out as the surrounding vegetation closes around it. The lack of competition will allow some native British orchids to grow far more vigorously in pot-culture than in the wild.

The Conservation of Orchids

Nowadays, strict national and international legislation has been formulated to protect and to control the trade in many species of wild orchid. We are well aware that some of the orchids we have treated in this book are rare in the wild and some are possibly threatened with extinction in some countries. We wish to make it quite clear that we abhor the removal of plants from the wild for transplantation to the garden. This practice, which is fortunately declining, is rarely successful. Furthermore, it is unnecessary as most of the plants we describe are already in cultivation where they are successfully propagated either from seed or by vegetative means, or are likely to become so in the near future following the research in orchid micropropagation that is being actively pursued in many countries at the present day.

The sad fate of the Lady's Slipper Orchid, *Cypripedium calceolus*, in the British Isles, illustrates only too graphically how gardeners can exterminate a species by their thoughtless activities or greed. This beautiful orchid was once found in many localities in a triangle from Derbyshire in the south to the Lake District and Northumberland in the north. By the middle of the last century it had already become a rarity and, early this century, Farrer was lamenting its imminent demise. By 1950 it had been reduced to a single locality where a few plants survived in a remote glen. Even these were dug up until only a single plant now remains. This is guarded day and night throughout the season to protect it from theft. It has been the sole survivor now for 40 years, a silent but poignant reminder of man's avarice and the potential fate of many of the world's most attractive flowers.

Sadly, *C.calceolus* is only one of many orchids that are gravely threatened now. Some orchids are so desirable and command such high prices that newly found colonies are stripped by dealers as soon as they are discovered. This happened to the spectacular Andean odontoglossums and Brazilian cattleyas in the last decades of the nineteenth century, and is happening today to the tropical relatives of the Lady's Slipper Orchid in South-East Asia and South and Central America. Indeed, two species of the South-East Asian slipper orchid genus *Paphiopedilum* are extinct in the wild now.

We believe that one way to protect our wild orchids is to learn how to grow them well in cultivation and to propagate them. Nursery-raised orchids grow much better than wild-collected ones. Furthermore, the most attractive and vigorous clones can be selected and bred from in cultivation, leading to the production of plants that have superior blooms and are more vigorous than their wild ancestors. Great advances have been made in the last few years in the propagation of orchids and this is equally as true of the hardy as it is of the tropical species. Many species considered previously to be impossible to grow can now be propagated. An Australian mycologist, Jack Warcup, reported in 1985 the successful flowering of the underground orchid, *Rhizanthella gardneri*, from seed less than two years from sowing. This remarkable feat, the first time a saprophytic species had been grown from seed and flowered in cultivation, demonstrates that nothing is impossible in orchid cultivation. A thorough understanding of the biology of the orchid underpins all such advances in cultivation. Support, therefore, the conservation-minded nurseryman raising his own stock. He will be your best hope of success in providing healthy vigorous plants.

Cultivation

Many approaches have been adopted in the cultivation of hardy orchids. Some are almost mandatory in order to grow certain groups, while others are a matter of choice according to one's circumstances or preference. A hardy orchid can be found for almost every situation. Some (albeit a minority) are garden plants which can be relied upon to grow and increase well, particularly in shady, mixed herbaceous or shrub/herbaceous borders, and woodland gardens. But, on the whole, orchids are plants for the specialist grower, who is prepared to take the time to understand their requirements, and to cater for them.

The success of numerous growers over the years has proved that terrestrial orchids are by no means as difficult to maintain as is generally believed. Hardy orchids have had limited success as garden plants, largely because they have been, on the whole, available only in small quantities. This,and their slow rate of vegetative increase, has led to hardy orchids being amongst the more expensive plants to purchase. That essential element of trial and error, which most gardeners require to master any novel group, has been something of a luxury. Thus they have remained largely the province of the connoisseur and plantsman.

Recent advances in the understanding of the requirements of hardy orchids, based upon a more sophisticated awareness of their biology and physiology, are now bringing them within the realm of the ordinary grower. The mass production of hardy orchids, some of which have proved quite difficult to grow using standard techniques developed for their exotic tropical cousins, is now being actively researched. Recent developments, such as the successful *in-vitro* symbiotic propagation from seed of tuberous terrestrial species (most hardy orchids fall in this group), should be seen alongside reports of vegetative multiplication *in vivo* of tuberous and rhizomatous terrestrials, as the harbinger of increased production, greater availability (and hopefully lower prices) for many hardy orchids.

How does one go about satisfying the requirements of hardy orchids, and in what ways do they differ from the more run-of-the-mill garden plants? A resumé of the main points of hardy orchid cultivation is given below.

PRINCIPLES OF ORCHID CULTIVATION

Whilst the two major sections of the orchid family, the epiphytes and terrestrials, may at first seem so vegetatively dissimilar, they do share to a great degree certain major requirements in cultivation. The same applies across the other great orchid divide, namely that between the tropical and temperate.

When cultivating orchids of all kinds, it is a very simple matter to 'kill with kindness'. With terrestrial orchids, the adaptations that enable them to withstand low-nutrient regimes, or periodic drought, are actually mandatory requirements. Many gardeners make the mistake of treating orchids exactly as they might other plants. Those with wider experience, such as alpine plant growers, can more readily understand that orchids may easily be over-cosseted.

Of course, most terrestrial orchids differ in important ways from their epiphytic cousins. The vast majority of those we deal with here have a definite dormancy period, when they have no parts above ground at all. Most are tuberous, or possess thin rhizomes. A few pseudobulbous genera have hardy members, for example *Cymbidium, Calanthe, Bletilla* and *Pleione*. The first two are also evergreen (*Calanthe* only partially so in severe seasons). The management of the dormant-season requirements of the plants is a critical factor, particularly when plants are being grown in containers. Despite their 'quasi-bulbous' nature, they are not as tough as the majority of other bulbous subjects.

'Ecological' growing methods

Here we turn to a subject which has been the cause of some contention, even controversy, in recent years. This is the division of terrestrial orchid growers into what may be termed pro- and anti- 'ecological' growing camps.

With the vast majority of terrestrial orchids, we have only recently moved on from considering them to be virtually uncultivable. However, well over a decade of successful culture of terrestrials from both hemispheres, particularly in Australia and Europe, has led to a dramatic revision of this 'received wisdom'. The success that has been achieved is mainly due to growers who have sought to understand the habitat requirements of terrestrial orchids and, in particular, their relationship with their mycorrhizal fungi. The division still remains, however, between those who believe in 'ecological' cultivation techniques designed to maintain and encourage mycorrhizal fungi, and those who do not. Certain American authors, speaking of their success with *Cypripedium* in particular, have claimed that the influence of mycorrhiza in their cultivation techniques is relatively limited.

However, our experience suggests that even mature plants of terrestrial orchids retain close relationships with mycorrhizal fungi. Almost all are characterised by considerably smaller root systems than those of other plants, which suggests that the orchids may still be benefitting from the ability of the fungi symbiont to forage for nutrients over a far larger area than that which the orchid roots occupy. Also, the methods employed by successful American growers have much in common with 'ecological' techniques, as we shall bring out later. It might be that a better understanding of the requirements of terrestrial orchids would allow them to be grown commercially as easily as are some of the epiphytes, in inert media with all nutrients supplied in their irrigation water. But for all practical purposes, and especially for the gardener, undoubtedly the best approach is to depend upon modifications of standard cultivation techniques. In order to cultivate any particular orchid, we must first discover what its requirements are, and how to meet them most easily. Is the plant we are looking at fully hardy under our conditions? Even if fully frost-hardy, would it benefit from protection from the extremes of frost and/or damp during the winter? Most growers hope to achieve the best results from their plants, which usually means providing optimal conditions. Therefore frame or alpine/glass house conditions may be required. Several key questions must be asked to be able to provide the best conditions for successful cultivation. Is the orchid in question terrestrial, or epiphytic? Very few epiphytic species are even half-hardy, but there are several that are very showy and desirable.

We must then consider the habitat of the plant in question — does it come from open or shady areas? Are conditions predominantly dry or wet during the growing and dormant seasons? Is the substrate in which it grows naturally acidic or alkaline, high or low in organic matter, well-drained or moisture-retentive? Another very important point is the provenance of the plant in question. This will be recognised by many growers of bulbous plants, which tend to come from habitats in which terrestrial orchids often abound (i.e. Mediterranean climates with hot dry summers and mild moist winters). Plants from these climates, whether European (especially lowland and mid-elevation species), Australian, South African or South American, all tend to be winter growers. This is an important factor in their cultivation, often indicating that they will demand some form of protection to obtain the best results.

Plants which come from higher elevations, or higher latitudes, are usually tougher, having to tolerate more severe winter conditions. But even with these species, relative hardiness can be deceptive. Take, for example, certain *Cypripedium* species from areas with cold winters with snow cover. Whilst they might well tolerate prolonged periods at very low temperatures, and indeed require some cold dormancy before they will initiate growth and flowering, they may be tricked into premature growth by the constantly changing conditions prevailing in oceanic climates, such as that of the British Isles. Encouraged into growth by mild spells in winter, they may then be damaged or killed by a subsequent return of severe weather. Here again, some form of protected cultivation may be required to obtain the best results.

This information is given under the account of each species in the Catalogue of orchids.

Habitat considerations and substrates/composts

The basic principles of orchid cultivation for the majority of orchids, terrestrial or epiphytic, are quite simple. Most of the orchids we grow appreciate an open, well-drained and aerated growing medium. Indeed, most orchids are very intolerant of stagnant conditions around their roots. The epiphytes have the greatest requirement for good aeration and drainage. Their root systems are usually very shallow, growing over or in thin layers of humus or moss. In many cases they may grow directly upon rocks or bark with no discernable substrate at all. Under these conditions the roots tolerate extremes of climate, even occasional drought. Although the habitats in which they are growing may at times be very wet, they will dry out very rapidly, and water does not linger around the roots for any length of time.

The epiphytic genera which we shall deal with here are principally tropical montane in origin, and include *Pleione, Dendrobium, Cymbidium* and *Coelogyne*. Whilst many species are not perhaps strictly epiphytic, it is the shared characteristics of these genera and their habitats which mean that they should be treated similarly in cultivation.

Other genera which can be treated similarly include *Bletilla* and *Calanthe*, again genera of tropical affinity.

Most terrestrial orchids also appreciate good drainage. This applies to species from open habitats, as well as most woodland species. A few terrestrials are associated with wet or boggy conditions, although scarcely two or three species can strictly be described as genuine semi-aquatic plants.

Those orchids which may grow in 'boggy' conditions include two horticulturally very important genera, *Cypripedium* and *Dactylorhiza*. Both contain species which will undoubtedly grow well in drier marginal 'bog garden' conditions. *Cypripedium*, in particular, has species which respond very well to being grown in artificial 'bogs', and we shall describe these later.

The other important point about orchid substrates is that they are invariably relatively poor in nutrients. Orchids are essentially poor-soil plants. Their ability to survive in impoverished soils or habitats, using the extended feeding system provided by their fungal symbionts, has equipped orchids to cope with such extreme conditions.

Epiphytes obtain little nourishment from the thin or non-existent 'soils' which characterise their habitats. Epiphytic orchids tend to have large, questing root systems, which serve the purpose of foraging over wide areas for nutrients, as well as simply anchoring the plant. It is interesting to note that terrestrial orchids usually have rather smaller root systems than other plants of a similar size perhaps due to their mycorrhizal relationship.

Orchids have evolved to make maximum use of the poor resources they have to hand. Almost all have some form of storage organ, whether the pseudobulb or succulent evergreen foliage of tropical genera, or the tuber and rhizome of the more familiar terrestrials. Most orchids have a life cycle which sees them making rapid vegetative growth when conditions are good, using the resources in their storage organs. Flowering may occur with the advent of new growth (especially with tropical epiphytes such as *Pleione* and *Coelogyne*). Other epiphytes make up their growths, and flower upon them during the dormant season, or as growth recommences (e.g. *Dendrobium*).

Many terrestrials, particularly the tuberous species (e.g. *Orchis, Ophrys, Serapias*), will flower towards the end of the vegetative growth phase, prior to entering into a dormant period to survive adverse conditions, whether dry and hot, or cold, Rhizomatous or pseudobulbous terrestrials tend to flower as they produce their new growths, e.g. *Cypripedium, Bletilla* and *Calanthe.*

ACCOMMODATING YOUR ORCHIDS

Orchids repay close attention. With a few notable exceptions, they are not plants to simply set out in the garden and forget! Some form of protection may need to be provided in order to obtain the optimal results from these fascinating plants. The types of orchids one can grow will, of course, be closely tied to the amount of protection given. But plants can be found for most situations.

Success with any specialist group of plants such as orchids, is dependent upon close control of growing conditions. Certain species will undoubtedly grow very well outside, such as the marsh orchids, *Dactylorhiza* and *Epipactis palustris*, but for the greatest success with the widest range of orchids, it is essential to grow them in containers in a glasshouse or frame. Whilst we are dealing with hardy orchids, i.e. those that will tolerate temperatures down to freezing, there is no doubt that protection from extremes of temperature, or winter wet, will produce considerable benefits for the majority of orchids in both productivity and quality of plants and flowers.

Let us, initially, consider orchids suitable for the open garden. There are many situations available in a garden where a strategically placed orchid will fit very well, and enhance the overall effect to provide a suggestion of the exotic.

Shady or woodland gardens

Undoubtedly, the finest and showiest garden orchids are to be found amongst those which grow in shady beds and borders, or woodland gardens.

Some of these will also do very well if grown in more open moist areas, as plants of the drier margins around water gardens. They may also be grown using the 'Holman Bog' (see below), or other methods which provide a cool root-run in open situations. Genera such as *Dactylorhiza*, *Epipactis* and *Cypripedium* have members which can grow in direct sunlight, given continual moisture around the roots.

At the Royal Horticultural Society's Garden at Wisley in England, it is possible to see the way in which a range of *Dactylorhiza* hybrids have established themselves from seed among water-garden marginal plantings. The parent plants were growing in the margins of a woodland garden. Plants appear to grow with equal vigour in both places, but flowering response seems better in lighter positions. These naturally spreading colonies effectively mimic the way in which the plants grow in drier parts of boggy areas in the wild.

Another good example of a plant which will grow well in a shady bed, and perhaps even better in a moist open situation, is *Cypripedium reginae*, one of the finest 'Lady's Slipper Orchids' for the garden. This probably reflects the plant's preference for a cool root-run, rather than its need for certain light conditions.

Shady borders

For the best conditions, a site which is indirectly shaded should be chosen. Overhead shade can be tolerated by most plants, but the drip from trees can lead to problems with damping-off of tender young growths. Avoid frost hollows at all costs, as considerable damage to newly emerging growths can occur due to late spring frosts. Gardeners with calcareous soils also face problems. Some species will thrive in them, given additional organic matter (e.g. *Cypripedium calceolus*), but for the majority of orchids, which grow in acid or neutral soils, raised beds will have to be built, preferably completely isolated from the limy conditions beneath. Layers of plastic with drainage holes to let excess water run away into non-alkaline drainage material beneath can provide a good solution to this problem.

If you cannot provide the dappled shade required by woodland garden plants, it may be possible to create your own 'woodland' by erecting a shade frame over a raised bed, on a north or eastern aspect. This has been done very effectively at the Royal Botanic Gardens at Kew, on the shady side of their Alpine House. The frame can be covered with a 50 per cent shadecloth, or with shade provided by laths, 13 mm wide ($^1/_2$ in), with a 13 mm ($^1/_2$ in) gap, again giving 50 per cent shade. Cloth has the advantage in that it can be removed easily when natural light is at a premium, from the autumn until the spring. In South-east England, shading is required from about late April until mid-September.

Whether growing in natural or artificial shade, the soil for the woodland garden should be made very open, and yet moisture-retentive, by the addition of good quantities of organic matter, preferably with some leafmould, although sphagnum or sedge peats are also appropriate. Many gardeners prefer to grow orchids in raised beds, using peat blocks, or stone (sandstone or other acidic rock for preference). Greater control over the soil conditions can be achieved, as one can backfill with exactly the soil required. As an added bonus the plants will also grow to a height where they may be more easily appreciated. A good soil mix for the woodland garden would consist of 40 per cent by bulk of leafmould and peat. The former will decay relatively quickly, giving nutrients as well as structure, whereas the latter will give longer-term structure to the soil. The other 60 per cent can be made up of 40 per cent loamy soil and 20 per cent sharp grit or coarse sand. The sand should be lime-free.

A base-dressing of fertiliser may be given. Incorporate hoof and horn at the same rate as recommended for potting media (10 ml per 10 litres, 1 dessertspoon per 2 gal). This can be renewed each year when top-dressing with fresh leafmould and peat, at the same rate.

Water will almost certainly be required from time to time, especially during spring, when even short periods of drought with drying winds can check growth severely. Soft water is best; those who have an alkaline water supply should use stored rain water if possible. The aim should be to retain some moisture in the soil at all times, in order that the humid microclimate the plants appreciate is continually maintained.

Marginal and bog gardens

These areas are usually in full sun, with continual moisture around the roots of the plants. The orchids which grow in such places greatly appreciate the cool root-run provided, but tend to root shallowly in the well-aerated upper layers, amongst humus mats, or mosses such as *Sphagnum*. Anaerobic or sour conditions around their roots will kill or damage orchids in these situations, as elsewhere.

When considering hardy orchids for these sites, we are limited to those which will grow in drier marginal areas. From applying this system of cultivation in the UK, and from the work of Holman and Beckner in the USA, the critical depth of unsaturated soil for the orchids to root into is 75–250 mm (3–10 in). This depth depends upon the species of orchid, its provenance and habitat. Below that, the substrate can be completely waterlogged. This will provide both a cool root-run, and continual reserves of moisture that the orchids can call on as required.

The 'Holman Bog' (Holman 1976) has been used with great success for hardy slipper orchids, especially as modified by Whitlow. Figure 6 shows the basic layout of the artificial bog area. *Cypripedium reginae* and *C. calceolus* var. *parviflorum* are best suited to this system. The actual construction is not especially arduous. A trench 300 mm (1 ft) deep is required. The length and width can be modified to suit the space available, although Holman originally used an area 1.2 m wide by 4.2 m long (4 ft × 14 ft). It should be in good light for much of the day, and certainly not heavily shaded.

The trench is lined with a polyethylene sheet, 4 or 6 microns thickness, attached to a hardwood frame 150 mm (6 in) deep, at a point half-way up. This leaves the top 75 mm (3 in) of the frame to drain either into the liner, or over the top and into the surrounding soil taken from the hole, mixed with organic matter (we would suggest sphagnum peat, to 25 per cent of the volume).

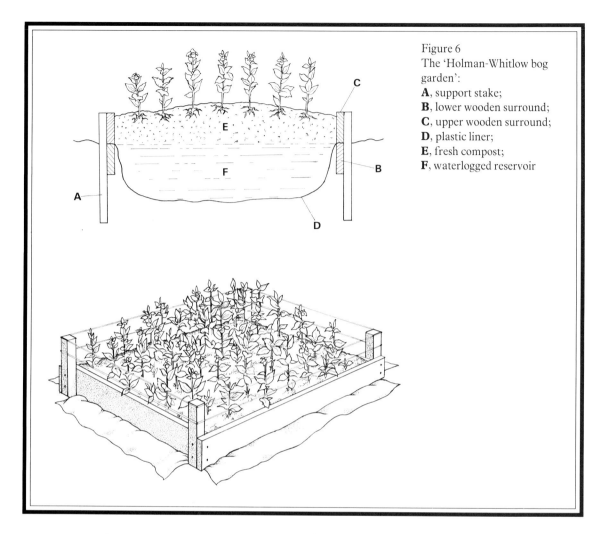

Figure 6
The 'Holman-Whitlow bog garden':
A, support stake;
B, lower wooden surround;
C, upper wooden surround;
D, plastic liner;
E, fresh compost;
F, waterlogged reservoir

Holman then filled the top 75 mm (3 in) with black lake-bottom peat from the area where the orchids grow. With our knowledge of how most orchids grow well in pots in standard composts, we would suggest that this is not critical, and that the top layer could equally well be filled with potting mix D (see p. 27) or the same mixture as we suggest for filling raised woodland garden beds (see p. 17).

The orchids are planted into this top layer, with their roots no more than 50 mm (2 in) deep. Over a period of four years the only further feeding and mulching that the beds needed was a layer of leaves heaped over the bed to a depth of about 300 mm (1 ft), at the end of each growing season. In Holman's artifical bog the plants thrived, increasing both vegetatively and in improved flowering, outperforming control populations observed in the wild. Conditions in the bog appeared quite stable, and watering was only required infrequently, not surprising when one considers that the water can only go one way, i.e. upwards!

The method described by Beckner (1979) is very similar, but he used large plastic containers, and the method will be discussed at greater length in the section on container growing (see p. 23).

Whitlow (1983) has also produced excellent results when growing *Cypripedium* in beds. He used a modified Holman Bog system to grow a wider range of species than Holman. Most plants were grown in conditions of open shade, with good light from a northerly aspect, although *C.reginae* and *C.candidum* could withstand full light, if grown with a cool moist root-run. The zone of permanent saturation in his 'bog' was 150–250 mm (6–10 in) below the surface of the soil, achieved by varying the depth of the plastic liner. Most of the species were kept at around the latter level above the water line.

For a bog with a slightly acid/neutral pH (derived from a mixture of garden soil and peat), he recommends *Cypripedium reginae, C.calceolus* (the European variety), *C.calceolus* var.*parviflorum, C.candidum, C.speciosum* and *C.macranthum* (as *C.hotei-atzumorianum*).

A more acid soil based upon pine duff and quartzite grit suited *Cypripedium formosanum, C.arietinum, C.guttatum, C.guttatum* var.*yatabeanum* and *C.cordigerum.* He succeeded in growing all of these species under his conditions in Iowa, and their cultivation can obviously be attempted using the artificial bog system without the necessity of creating woodland garden conditions.

Whitlow recommends fertilising the beds, using a general fertiliser at one-tenth of its recommended concentration. It may be that this would be best applied as a foliar feed, which we have seen can be beneficial to orchids, without the problems that may be encountered from artificial fertilisers in 'ecological' growing systems.

One of the great merits of using artificial bogs is that they may be set up anywhere, for example in a small patch of border alongside a greenhouse. They provide very specialised growing conditions with minimal maintenance requirements, when compared to pot-culture. The success of the species tried suggests that other species might also respond to this method of cultivation.

Orchids for other outdoor situations

A number of species can be accomodated in beds and borders, although they tend to require some modification of the soil to suit their requirements. The same technique applies to planting in pockets of soil in the rock garden.

Orchids are not necessarily good competitors with other herbaceous garden plants and are best suited to areas where the other vegetation is not too exuberant. Ideal sites include warm sunny borders immediately next to a house or greenhouse wall, where the more tender species may be tried in positions which offer some protection from the worst the winter can throw at them. Even here, the extra protection afforded by a pane of glass or tile over the plant during the wettest part of the year may be of benefit.

Many species will grow well in the sunny dry garden, or in scree areas. Those who garden on chalky soils can provide near perfect conditions quite easily for a few choice tuberous species. Many tuberous terrestrials which are grown outdoors, do in fact come from seasonally dry Mediterranean climates, and even their northern outliers in genera such as *Ophrys* and *Orchis* will not complain, if given the same conditions as those for their more southerly cousins. It naturally follows that they are also good subjects for troughs and sink gardens, where their requirements can be more or less exactly catered for, and they are protected to some degree from pests and poor drainage. This, however, is really a modified form of container growing, and will be discussed under that heading (see p.22).

Modifying the soil

Tuber-bearing species should always be provided with a well-drained position. As with the woodland species, avoid frost pockets, or early growths may be nipped back. The soil should be more-or-less similar in structure to that used in containers. Clay soils require lightening with sand and organic matter, and sandy soils should have loam and organic matter added to them, to obtain that elusive medium loam structure. Compost C may be used (see p.27) to provide an area of soil entirely suited to orchids.

A quantity of sharp gritty sand can be incorporated both into the area where the orchids are planted, and around the 'neck' of the plant to ensure immediate drainage of water around the plants, and good quantities of air at a point where many disease problems can arise. These techniques are quite typical of those employed by many bulb and alpine plant growers. A top-dressing of gravel, small granite or dolomite chips or other material as preferred aesthetically or suggested by the habitats of the plants, can be provided with some benefit.

A number of species can be tried outdoors in dry beds with realistic hopes of success. Those gardening on limy soils might try *Anacamptis pyramidalis* and *Gymnadenia conopsea*. If your soil is acidic, incorporate dolomite limestone into the planting area, and perhaps top-dress with dolomite chippings also. *Ophrys* species may also be grown in alkaline soils, but are rather more demanding, and may only thrive for a relatively brief period. *O.sphegodes* and *O.apifera* have been known to grow well in such situations. It is advisable only to experiment when one has sufficient stock to bear any losses with equanimity!

Another genus with a number of species worthy of consideration for the garden is *Orchis*. *O.morio* and *O.mascula* are both native to Britain, which means that they will be more suited to colder winters. Another (albeit less showy) species which will do well is *Aceras anthropophorum*.

Moving away from tuberous species, the autumn-flowering *Spiranthes spiralis* will grow well in pockets in the rock garden with a neutral-alkaline soil, extending the flowering season. Perhaps the most rewarding orchid, in terms of both its attractive flowers and its ease of culture in particular, is the Hyacinth Orchid, *Bletilla striata*. This can form quite large clumps in borders which receive some shade, especially greenhouse borders. If surrounded by non-invasive neighbours, it will even be accommodating enough to grow in the shadier section of the herbaceous and mixed shrub/herbaceous border. A neutral-acid soil, with added organic matter, suits this species best. In cooler parts of the British Isles or during periods of especially intense cold, protection with straw or some other loose organic matter heaped over the crowns will ensure its survival. The flowers are an attractive magenta, but pale lavender and pure white forms are also available.

Of all garden orchids, the Hyacinth Orchid is the best for beginners to try. However, if bought as dry rhizomes, plants should spend their first year in a pot, where they can build up their strength in readiness for the world outside. They should be planted in the spring, when danger of frost has passed, to enable them to settle in well over their first growing season. Thereafter they should be very dependable, and should increase readily, especially if planted in the border.

Orchids in frames and greenhouses

The majority of the orchids dealt with here should be housed in frames or greenhouses for optimal results. Whilst most, if not all, will undoubtedly survive the occasional frost, and can thus be broadly described as hardy, the results using some form of protection will usually surpass those from growing in the open, in the conditions prevailing in the British Isles.

The best form of protection is that provided by the classic alpine house, well ventilated, kept at ambient temperatures in summer, and cool but not freezing in winter. In his seminal work *Collectors' Alpines*, Royton Heath describes the shock of the 'purist' alpine plant growers, when they learned that he grew his plants with enough heat to prevent freezing of the containers. This treatment is essential for potted plants, and more so for those that grow in winter, such as the majority of Mediterranean terrestrial orchids. If frozen solid at the roots, these plants can be swiftly desiccated by high day temperatures at the plant surface on a sunny clear (and outside, cold) winter's day, because the plant will attempt to draw water up from a frozen substrate (an impossibility!). Subsequent stress in the plant can lead to problems.

The night minimum which should be maintained to ensure this problem does not occur is 1°C 34°F). Whatever form of heater is used, it should have a sensitive thermostatic controller, capable of maintaining that temperature to within 1°C (1.8°F). Electric fan heaters, with a remote thermostat set at pot level, are appropriate for this purpose. A further benefit of these is that the air movement will dry the foliage, lessening the chance of fungal or bacterial attack.

Temperatures may occasionally dip below the recommended minimum, but as long as the plants are not allowed to freeze solid, little harm should befall them. The setting of the thermostat should be checked against a maximum/minimum thermometer, again set at plant level, which will provide a useful guide as to whether or not the desired temperatures are being maintained. A day lift of around 2°C (4–5°F) will be of benefit to the growth of the plants, especially when conditions outside the greenhouse do not allow for any appreciable solar gain.

Should one wish to maintain the widest selection of hardy orchids, spreading perhaps into the Australian terrestrials and hardier epiphytes (the hardier species and hybrids of *Pleione* excepted), then a higher minimum temperature, of between 4–5°C (38–40°F) is preferable. This temperature will also suit the less hardy autumn-flowering pleiones. A further benefit of maintaining this temperature regime is that many plants will grow steadily throughout the winter, and the flowering season in a collection can be greatly enhanced. To take an example, in the Kew collection we have seen clones of *Orchis papilionacea* flower from December through until early April, depending on provenance. Under cold conditions they may restrict their flowering to the spring period alone. Most growers will well appreciate the value of flowers in December and January, and there are numerous choice plants to provide colour at this otherwise dreary time of year.

Frame cultivation

Frames can be sited in several different ways. They may stand alone, with no protection from cold temperatures, in full sun for those species which demand a high light regime. For more protection they can be placed against a wall, in a place chosen to provide conditions that suit the plants being grown. Thus frames on north- and east-facing walls will suit woodland plants, whilst those facing south and west will house plants which appreciate higher light to full sun. Frames alongside a greenhouse may benefit more directly from the heat in the house, by having box ventilators or air bricks set in the shared wall to allow warmer air into the frame.

The standard bulb frame serves two purposes, offering dry conditions for the summer dormancy of the majority of its hardy inhabitants, and

protecting them from the extremes of winter wet and cold. Plants may be grown in a suitable special compost which fills the frame (or sections of it), or otherwise in containers, which in a completely unheated frame should be plunged, to protect their contents from freezing.

These conditions will undoubtedly suit some of the hardier winter-growing terrestrials very well. At Kew we have seen the colony-forming *Serapias olbia* thriving when planted into an outside frame. Under exceptionally severe winter conditions the frame may be covered with sacking, to prevent excessive freezing within. Otherwise, the frame and its contents require light, airy conditions. Some form of ventilation is necessary for most of the winter, to prevent build-up of humidity.

In spring and summer the bulb frame will require no side glass at all, just the roof glass to protect the contents from rain. This is not to say that the frame should remain entirely unwatered for the summer period, as dormant orchids in particular can become excessively desiccated. Occasional waterings to maintain some moisture in the compost effectively mimic their natural habitat, where occasional storms will provide some back-up to the soil moisture. It must also be borne in mind that in open situations most terrestrial orchid tubers and rhizomes are protected by the residual moisture in the soil from the sort of desiccation that can occur in frames and containers.

Frames alongside walls and glasshouses, designed to house the more shade-loving terrestrials, may have their tops removed for the summer period, and be completely open to the elements. If the aspect of the frame is not quite right, and shading is required, it can be provided by shadecloth stretched across a framework over the frame or 13 mm (½ in) laths with a 13 cm (½ in) gap on a frame tailored to fit.

We recommend using the same compost for growing orchids *in situ* in the frame as that suggested for growing these orchids in containers (see below).

Growing hardy orchids in a glasshouse

Hardy orchids can be accommodated all the year round in a glasshouse, or may spend part of their time in outside frames, to be brought inside when in flower. At Kew, we have grown a very wide range of hardy species, both from southern and northern latitudes (i.e. winter and summer growers together), in the same house for a number of years, with good results. There is no reason why, for example, northern *Cypripedium* species cannot grow alongside Mediterranean *Ophrys* and *Orchis*, as the conditions which the former require in winter (i.e. cool dormancy with the night temperatures dipping to around 1–3°C (34–38°F)), suit the growth of the latter. Summer glasshouse conditions in the classical alpine house, with ambient temperatures, side and ridge ventilation, light shading (up to 50 per cent), and a reasonable relative humidity (50–60 per cent), have proved perfect for the dormancy of the winter-growing terrestrials, providing the appropriate rest without stress.

The combination of glasshouse and frames allows the greatest flexibility, with the cool conditions enjoyed or demanded by the hardiest genera easy to provide in unheated frames outside the glasshouse. The flowering season of genera such as *Pleione* can also be extended, using the combination of frames and glasshouse, by keeping plants cool until they might be brought into the house to flower. The flowering of many plants can be extended in this way; for example, those species of *Cypripedium* which, like *C. acaule*, flower within a very short period of being brought into warmer conditions.

The classic alpine house may be the ideal, but it is by no means impossible to provide conditions to suit a wide range of terrestrials in a more basic structure. Particular attention must be paid to ventilation and shading, to provide optimal conditions throughout the year. Something approaching 50 per cent ridge and side ventilation should suffice, when used with shade cloth or laths on a framework between 250–500 mm (10–20 in) above the glass. This gap provides much needed insulation from a layer of still air between the shading and the glass, which is particularly important in a small structure. Any glass doors may also be replaced during summer with a coarse mesh shadecloth stretched across a frame, letting air in, and keeping animals and birds out.

To buffer pots and root systems against sudden fluctuations in temperature, and to cut down on water loss through clay containers, many alpine plant growers plunge their pots to the rim in a bed of sharp sand. Whilst this can be done with orchids, we would counsel that they are best grown on slatted or other open stagings, much as their tropical counterparts are. This allows for immediate drainage of water from the pot, improves aeration, and prevents the spread of water-borne pathogens from pot to pot through the moisture in the plunge bed. Whilst this necessitates extra attention in watering, it does effectively remove one method by which diseases may spread, as well as preventing rooting into the sand, which can lead to damage to any roots which have left the container, when the plant is moved.

During the summer, the relative humidity within the house should be increased on hot, still days. This can be done by regularly wetting the floor, or by installing a simple mist line system beneath the benches, controlled by a timer switch or humidistat and solenoid valve. Shading is necessary from early April until September in southern England, maybe a fortnight later farther north.

The management of the environment to suit orchids in the normal cool alpine house is quite straightforward, and they do fit in very well with the regime suitable for the great majority of other alpines. Given the benefits of growing in glasshouses, and the relatively small cost of maintaining ideal temperatures for many orchids, glasshouse culture has everything to recommend it. If growing a selection of plants which require extra heat, say to 4–5°C night minimum (around 40°F), a special section can be partitioned off in the house, and extra heat provided without being detrimental to other alpine plants which demand colder conditions.

Growing orchids in containers

Container growing techniques provide the greatest control of the conditions in any orchid collection. These are best used in conjunction with protected cultivation in frames or glasshouses. The basic aim of container growing is to provide a root environment for the plants which is completely under the control of the grower.

Under the heading of container growing we will deal with everything from cultivation in plastic pots, troughs and sink gardens, to the American 'mini-bogs', which have been successfully employed for some of their previously 'uncultivable' wetland species.

Types of container

Many growers have very strong opinions as to what type of containers best 'suit' orchids. For many years tradition ruled that epiphytic orchids could not be grown in plastic pots, because of their need of well-aerated conditions at the roots, more easily obtained in the more porous clay pots used for generations. This myth has taken some time to break down, but it is now generally accepted that it is the management of the compost and the plants in the container provided which is critical, rather than the type of container chosen.

Orchids, terrestrial or otherwise, can be grown in many different types of container. Many alpine plant growers set out to create miniature landscapes, or mini-habitats in troughs and sink gardens. Such conditions suit orchids well, given the correct soil type, and non-competitive neighbours. The odd corner, for example, of a trough or raised bed devoted to acid-loving plants may be greatly enhanced in spring by a *Calanthe* or *Cypripedium*. The same applies to growing orchids from alkaline conditions in a trough devoted to other calcicole plants. As troughs can be moved into sheltered areas during severe weather, more tender species may be grown in them.

See p. 27, below, for the types of compost required for orchids growing in these situations.

Growing bog orchids in containers

The basic sink garden or trough is well understood by most growers. The creation of bog conditions in miniature is rather more of a novelty, and the fact that under such conditions orchids might thrive, is something which appears to go against most of the basic principles of orchid growing. However, for the majority of 'bog' orchids, the most critical aspect is the creation of a microhabitat, wherein the plants with which bog orchids are associated, particularly sphagnum mosses, will do well.

This style of growing has been pioneered by the carnivorous plant growing fraternity, and those in the USA who have evolved the system do indeed use carnivorous plants (which naturally abound in many bog orchid habitats), as companion plants to the orchids. As will be seen from the basic methods detailed below, with one or two exceptions, the orchids are actually growing in open, moist, well-aerated and highly organic substrates, well above the zone of permanent saturation, in conditions that very effectively mimic those of their natural habitats. These systems therefore take into account the ecology of the plants in question.

Certain genera, particularly *Cypripedium* from wetter habitats, appear to have benefited greatly from growing under artificial 'bog' conditions, both in containers and in beds. Their requirements can be provided when grown in standard containers in a frame or glasshouse, but greater attention to watering is then undoubtedly necessary, so the merits of growing in an artificial bog deserve close attention.

We have found that the American species *Spiranthes cernua* var. *odorata* will certainly grow in a wide variety of conditions, either directly in water (given a marginal position to establish itself in), in pots with a saturated zone in a clay loam-based compost, or in pots with normal drainage, given a retentive organic compost and more regular watering. This suggests that a number of 'bog' species may be amenable to differing approaches, as long as their basic requirements for an overall moist root-run are respected. These species are probably the minority, however, and certainly most seem more at home in the conditions described below.

Beckner's (1979) growing methods are those which appear to suit the widest variety of bog orchids. Plastic containers without drainage holes can be used. Beckner suggests that orchids prefer large containers (in fact up to and including paddling pools!), and no less than 200 mm (8 in) deep. A zone of permanently saturated medium to within 75 mm (3 in) of the top is created. A few short narrow slits in the side of the container at that level are provided to allow for drainage of excess water. A further 50 mm (2 in) of planting medium is then placed above this, and the top 25 mm (1 in) is finished off with living *Sphagnum* moss.

The containers should be set in an area which receives full sun for most of the day, and is fully open to the air. Beckner suggests that they should also be fully exposed to the winter cold, but as the plants in question were being grown in Florida, that is a relative cold, and in more northerly latitudes it would be wise to ensure that the containers did not freeze solid.

The growing medium suggested by Beckner consists of 5 parts perlite, 3 parts vermiculite and 2 parts sphagnum moss peat. Planting is done by spreading the orchid roots over the surface of this medium (which it will be remembered ended 25 mm (1 in) below the surface of the container), with the whole thing being finished off by living *Sphagnum* carefully placed around the plants to keep them upright whilst they establish. The planting height may be varied to suit the plants in question. Those which appreciate wetter conditions may be placed lower, closer to the saturated area (e.g. *Spiranthes cernua* var. *odorata*), and those that grow under drier conditions higher (e.g. *Pogonia*).

All watering must be done with rain water. If tap or other water is used it must be softened prior to use. No fertilisers at all are used in this system (*Sphagnum*, like many orchids, is most intolerant of mineral fertilisers). Once the *Sphagnum* is established and growing well, the health of the orchids seems to be assured. Genera such as *Spiranthes*, *Pogonia*, *Platanthera*, *Cleistes* and *Calopogon* thrive under this regime. It can be surmised that good results should be obtained with many other orchids from other parts of the world which share this habitat.

Growing orchids in pots

Terrestrial orchids appreciate a more even moisture regime within the pot than their epiphytic cousins, allowing their mycorrhizal fungi to thrive. Thus we would suggest that terrestrials are best grown in plastic, rather than clay containers. We do not suggest that they will not grow in clay pots,

and, if one's preference is for those, then by all means use them. Clay pots do, however, dry more rapidly than plastic. Thus we would recommend potting in a clay container perhaps a size larger than one would do if using less porous plastic pots. Checking for watering will also have to be more frequent. On the positive side, clay pots will certainly give a greater margin of error if one is by nature an over-waterer. Plastic pots are cheaper nowadays, and generally more readily available. Wherever possible, use one type of container throughout the collection. This makes checking for watering much simpler, as the pots will tend to dry at a similar rate. It is important also to ensure that plastic containers have sufficient drainage holes, both to shed water and to provide extra aeration. For safety, a few extra drainage holes bored into the base of the pot are recommended.

Container size

Conventional wisdom used to have it that orchids should be potted in small containers. For epiphytes, this overcame the frequent problem of over-watering, and for terrestrials, it seemed to follow on naturally from their rather small root systems. However, it is now accepted that a larger pot, with its more stable and even conditions within, is preferable. The larger pot also gives a greater volume of compost for the mycorrhizal fungi to utilise. A danger always exists, however, that poor watering technique will lead to larger pots becoming waterlogged. This is one of the reasons behind the emphasis we give to the structure of orchid composts, which must be sufficiently open and well-aerated to dry readily, as the dynamics of a relatively small plant in a comparatively large pot require careful management.

The absolute minimum pot size for mature terrestrial orchid plants, whether plastic or clay, should be 100 mm (4 in). Smaller pots tend to dry very quickly, and thus do not provide the stable root environment which is of great importance for the orchids and their mycorrhizal fungi to thrive. For preference, particularly for larger species, and when growing more than one plant in a pot, a container of 125–150 mm (5–6 in) and upwards should be chosen. In our experience, we have found broad-based 'squat' pots, or half pots, to be preferable, with their greater surface area to compost ratio, which is of importance in aeration and drying.

The majority of terrestrial and epiphytic orchids should be repotted every year. There are exceptions, notably the rhizomatous species, which tend to resent such regular disturbance. Genera such as *Cypripedium* will thrive for a number of years in the same container, with regular top-dressings to provide extra nourishment. These should, therefore, be potted in a container large enough to provide room for several years' growth. The minimum size should be 150 mm (6 in) for a small division, while larger mature plants can be quite magnificent in pots of 250–400 mm (10–16 in) and upwards.

ORCHID COMPOSTS

Perhaps one of the most difficult things to explain to an international readership, is the thorny question of just what exactly makes up a good compost. Numerous problems of both language (technical and trade terms understandable in one country meaning little to growers in another), and the ever present problem of availability of ingredients, aggravate this situation. The provision of composts suitable for a diverse collection of terrestrial orchids in particular, each growing in nature in different local soils and conditions, can multiply these problems considerably. However, experience at Kew, over a number of years of maintaining a diverse terrestrial collection from all parts of the world, has shown that a great range of species can be grown in a relatively small number of basic composts, with modifications provided for certain genera and species where appropriate.

The critical nature of terrestrial orchid composts has much to do with the desire to maintain the fungal symbiont alongside the orchid. Epiphytes are much more tolerant and will thrive in a wide range of composts, given that they provide the correct structure for the plants in question. We shall deal first with the epiphytes, after a brief discussion of terms to be used.

Loam: As applied to potting composts, loam is derived from turf taken from the top 75–100 mm (3–4 in) of a pasture, or other area put down to grass. This turf is then stacked and allowed to rot. The resultant material is a mixture of well-structured soil and some fibrous organic matter. The soil fraction, for a good loam, should consist of both clay and sand, the former to keep moisture and minerals, and the latter to keep the soil open to drainage and aeration. Loam is usually sterilised prior to use. For orchids, steam or heat sterilisation only should be used (rather than chemical means, which may leave residues that can adversely affect the mycorrhizal fungi).

Loam, as generally understood, is neither very heavy or very light (i.e. without too great a clay or sand fraction). Nor does it contain excessive undecayed organic matter such as peat. Loam is not usually taken from calcareous soils (i.e. those with a high pH.).

Many terrestrial orchid growers may wish to substitute garden soil for loam. This is obviously a far more variable product! But if it is well-structured, and free of pathogens and noxious weeds, it may be suitable. A 'rule of thumb', to gain some idea of the status of one's own soil, is to squeeze a handful of moist soil quite tightly. If it all sticks together, it is probably high in clay (and would need opening up with sand and organic matter). If it just holds together, showing signs of breaking apart into distinct 'crumbs', then it is a medium loamy soil. Soil that simply falls apart after this treatment is sandy.

Sand: In terrestrial orchid growing, sand is a very important compost ingredient. It helps to keep the compost open, and in drainage of surplus water. Orchid growers should always use sharp sand, and for preference it should contain considerable quantities of particles which are of around 4–7 mm ($\frac{1}{8}$–$\frac{1}{4}$ in) diameter. Crushed quartzite grit is particularly good for this purpose.

Leafmould: Leaves decayed to the point where they readily break down into small particles constitute leafmould. In terrestrial orchid composts, leafmould provides nourishment to the plant in two ways: directly by its own decay, and indirectly by being broken down by the mycorrhizal hyphae, which then pass on the nutrients to the orchids. It also serves the purpose of retaining moisture, and assisting in keeping the compost open, until it decays. The type of leafmould available to growers will, of course, depend on where they live. In Europe and much of North America, leafmould derived from oak, beech, hornbeam or birch is most suitable. For species from areas where coniferous forests predominate, 'pine duff' (partially decayed pine or other coniferous needles) is equally useful.

In Australia and New Zealand, leafmould may be derived from the genera which grow in the areas where the orchids grow, such as *Eucalyptus*, *Nothofagus*, etc. Australian species have done well for many years at Kew when grown with 'Northern hemisphere' leafmould, which would appear to be to the taste of their Australian mycorrhizae!

Peat: Sphagnum moss peat has replaced leafmould in composts for most practical purposes, although for orchids the latter is preferable. Its properties are mainly structural, retaining water and keeping the compost open, until it decays. Sphagnum peat derives from Sphagnum bogs. It is acidic in character, and for preference retains some of its fibrous structure (i.e. not milled excessively fine). A medium or coarse peat, passed through a 13 mm ($1/2$ in) sieve, should provide the sort of material which admirably suits orchids. Some peats may be alkaline in character, and are thus unsuitable for some species. Sedge peats tend to decay very rapidly, so should be avoided unless there are no alternatives.

Bark: Two major types are most suitable for our purposes, both derived from chipped conifer bark (particularly pine bark). Matured, but essentially undecayed, orchid bark should be used for epiphytes, as it has particularly long-lasting structural qualities. For terrestrials we have found that partially-decayed 'composted' bark, as supplied for general use in potting composts, is very useful. This material will have lost most of its more volatile chemicals, which might adversely affect the orchid roots and symbiotic fungi, and will decay more readily in the compost.

Epiphytic orchid composts

For the genera *Pleione*, *Cymbidium* and *Dendrobium*, and also *Bletilla* and *Calanthe*, there are two approaches to maintaining them in a hardy orchid collection. One may use the same type of compost as specialist tropical orchid growers, based upon chipped bark; alternatively, a modified terrestrial mix based upon a mixture of sand, loam (or soil), peat, moss and leafmould may be used. Each is quite different in its qualities. The former is less retentive, losing water to drainage and drying out rapidly, and without the nutrient availability of soil/leafmould-based composts. This is partly due to the nature of its ingredients, as they are not naturally rich in plant nutrients, and also because bark which has not been composted tends to rob potting composts of nutrients, due to the activities of the fungi and bacteria which decay it.

Both, however, can produce equally satisfactory results. It has to be borne in mind that in epiphytic orchid composts, under-watering is a danger while they are still fresh, whereas terrestrial mixes may easily be over-retentive for epiphytic orchids, unless watered with care.

Compost A:
'Orchid grower's' epiphyte mix

6 parts medium-grade orchid bark
3 parts chopped sphagnum moss (or fibrous sphagnum moss peat)
1 part 'supercoarse' perlite
1 part medium-grade charcoal
2 parts mixed beech/oak leafmould (passed through a 13 mm ($1/2$ in) sieve)

Compost B:
Soil-based epiphyte mix

6 parts fibrous loam (heat sterilised)
3 parts chopped sphagnum moss (or fibrous sphagnum moss peat)
3 parts 'supercoarse' perlite or coarse crushed grit (6 mm ($1/4$ in) size)
1 part medium-grade charcoal
2 parts mixed beech/oak leafmould (passed through a 13 mm ($1/2$ in) sieve)

The fibrous loam fraction in the soil-based mix is mandatory; if it cannot be obtained the orchid grower's mix is preferable. Garden soil is a dangerous thing to have anywhere near true epiphytes!

Terrestrial orchid composts

A great variety of terrestrial orchids can be grown from all over the world. European genera such as *Orchis, Dactylorhiza* and *Ophrys* can be cultivated side by side with Australasian genera such as *Pterostylis, Corybas,* and *Thelymitra.* All have species which grow well in a frost-free glasshouse, and the hardier disas from South Africa can also be accommodated at the upper end of the temperature range.

North American species in genera such as *Platanthera, Spiranthes* and *Cypripedium* have a proven track record in cultivation, and there are many other exciting North American terrestrials which should also prove to be suitable subjects, but unfortunately are not yet commercially available in Britain. From the American terrestrials it is but a short step to the cypripediums, calanthes, cymbidiums and numerous other cold-growing genera from Japan through China to Tibet, north Burma, Nepal and North India.

Such a selection of the world's temperate habitats should, and does, suggest a considerable range of conditions under which these plants grow naturally. However, for cultural purposes terrestrials from the northern hemisphere can broadly be divided into two categories: those that grow in open habitats and those from woodland. A third compost is needed for the Southern Hemisphere Australian species, and the South African disas require a compost which differs radically from the normal terrestrial mix.

But the similarities in terrestrial orchid composts outweigh the differences to a great degree. Rather than give a great number of slightly different mixes, three basic composts are given below, each of which can be amended to suit the particular needs of each species as described in the Catalogue. A fourth mix for disas is also given.

Compost C:
Basic terrestrial mix

(This compost suits a very wide range of terrestrials, from Europe, North America and Asia.)

3 parts heat-sterilised loam
3 parts coarse gritty sand or crushed grit (6 mm ($^1/_4$ in) size)
2 parts beech/oak leafmould (passed through a 13 mm ($^1/_2$ in) sieve
1 part composted pine bark (6mm ($^1/_4$ in) size)
Base-dressing of hoof and horn meal at 10 ml per 10 litre (1 dessertspoon per 2 gal).

Compost D:
Woodland terrestrial mix

(For woodland genera such as *Cypripedium* and *Calanthe,* as well as those species which grow in more moist areas, such as dactylorhizas from boggy habitats.)

2 parts heat-sterilised loam
2 parts beech/oak leafmould (passed through a 13 mm ($^1/_2$ in) sieve)
1 part fibrous sphagnum moss peat
1 part sharp sand or crushed grit (6 mm ($^1/_4$ in) size)
Base-dressing of hoof and horn meal at 10 ml per 10 litres (1 dessertspoon per 2 gallons).

Compost E:
Australasian terrestrial mix

(This mix suits the more specialised requirements of species from Australia in particular, and is based on those widely used there.)

2 parts coarse gritty sand
1 part heat-sterilised loam
1 part 'buzzer chips' (untreated hardwood or softwood chippings from sawmills), or bark chippings 6 mm ($^1/_4$ in) size
Plus fertiliser, blood and bonemeal 10 ml per 10 litre bucket of mix (approx. 1 dessertspoon per 2 gal).

Compost F:
Disa mix

In the wild, the evergreen disas which we deal with in this book (typified by *Disa uniflora*), may grow in substrates ranging from peat to pure sand, frequently by running (and therefore well-aerated) water. Their substrates are always very low in nutrients, with a very acid pH. Disas have been grown very well using modified hydroponic techniques, for example by running water along channels with living *Sphagnum* moss growing in them, and establishing the plants in the moss. Pure sand composts have also been used with success, but for ease of cultivation we have found composts based upon sphagnum moss peat and perlite to be the best, being both open and well-aerated. The peat should be of a medium grade, and not broken down finely, or it will decay too rapidly and clog the pore spaces in the compost. No base-dressings are required. The *Disa* mix consists of:

2 parts medium-grade sphagnum moss peat
1 part 'supercoarse' grade perlite

Note that where base-dressings of fertiliser are recommended for tuberous terrestrials, they consist solely of organically derived materials. Recent research has suggested that inorganic fertiliser salts can adversely affect mycorrhizal fungi. All of the mixes above are basically acidic. Should plants from alkaline areas be grown, a further base-dressing of dolomite limestone should be incorporated, at 20 ml per 10 litre of mix (2 dessertspoon per 2 gal).

Rockwool for orchids

Commercially important groups of orchids, particularly the tropical epiphytes which form the major part of the pot plant and cut flower trade, have been grown successfully in rockwool for a number of years. Rockwool itself is a product derived from molten volcanic rock, spun at very high speed to produce a medium similar to the fibreglass used in insulation. It has qualities as an orchid medium which suit it ideally to epiphytes. In particular, it holds a large amount of air, even when fully charged with water. Thus orchid roots can enjoy well-aerated and moist conditions simultaneously. Rockwool retains its structure for a number of years, avoiding the problems with organic media (which lose their structure quite

rapidly as they age) and so considerably lengthening the time between repotting. The disturbance of repotting is also greatly reduced, as plants in rockwool are 'dropped on', rather than stripped of all old compost.

Rockwool is chemically inert, and takes on the pH and salt concentrations of the water used to irrigate it. This means that growers must provide all the nutrients that plants growing in rockwool require, at the correct concentrations for optimal growth. Due to the qualities of rockwool, however, it is far easier to monitor the conditions in which the plants are growing, using relatively cheap meters to assess both pH and salt concentrations. Commercial growers can use sophisticated dilutors for feeding, and amateur growers are now being offered a number of systems designed specifically for orchids, using fertilisers formulated for the medium.

The use of rockwool for commercially important orchids shows that the system is perfectly appropriate for epiphytes; indeed it appears to be more productive than the standard organic media-based growing systems in use for many years. Initial research into using rockwool for tuberous terrestrial orchids shows that the system may well be appropriate for that group also. This area of research is in its early stages, but holds the promise of a simplified growing system for terrestrial orchids in the future.

POTTING

For potting purposes, orchids can be separated into three major groups: the epiphytes; the rhizomatous terrestrial genera; and the tuberous terrestrials. In common with other plants, most orchids are best repotted during their dormancy, typically as they are just about to re-start into growth. One or two interesting exceptions to this broad rule will be mentioned as necessary.

Dormancy in orchids varies considerably. Those from higher latitudes and altitudes are winter dormant, whereas those from Mediterranean climates, and the southern hemisphere, tend to become dormant during the summer dry season. Epiphytic species from the tropics also make up their growths in the summer, whilst they might flower during their vegetative dormancy, in the winter.

We shall deal with each of the major groups separately, beginning with the ephiphytes; very much the minority, but with a special role in providing flamboyant blooms in the cold and cool greenhouse.

Potting epiphytes

Before considering how to pot epiphytes, we must also consider why it is necessary — deciding whether they might need regular repotting at all. Most of the orchids dealt with in this work should be repotted annually to maintain optimal growing conditions for the orchids and their mycorrhizal fungi. We have already mentioned that epiphytic orchids are more amenable to cultivation, and that the needs of their symbionts are not as critical. The structure and condition of the compost is all-important in deciding whether or not to repot epiphytes.

We would suggest that epiphytes grown in loam-based mixes should certainly be repotted every year, because of the likelihood that the compost will lose its structure quite rapidly after the first season. Unless very carefully handled, epiphytes in poorly structured media will rapidly succumb to root rots, while new roots will not grow into poorly structured compost.

Bark-based potting media are often longer-lived, if prepared with good quality materials and handled correctly. Two, or even three, years' pot-life may then be obtained, but they should be checked every year to ensure that they are in good condition. Do not make decisions about repotting based upon the condition of the top of the compost, as decomposition will have been much more rapid in the moister conditions below. Checking this entails carefully removing the root-ball from the pot, as the loose structure of bark composts means that they may fall apart easily when taken out of the pot. If the structure can still be clearly seen to provide open channels for the passage of air and water through the mix, the compost smells 'sweet' and the individual particles of bark are not badly decomposed, then it may

well be that another year's growth can be obtained from it.

This lack of disturbance can sometimes be of benefit in obtaining specimen plants, especially with genera such as *Pleione*.

How to pot

Epiphytes for the cold or cool greenhouse fall into two distinct groups: the rhizomatous species, such as *Dendrobium*; and *Pleione*, with its distinctive growth habit, producing annual pseudobulbs. In the wild all epiphytes grow with their rhizomes, and much of their root systems, at or very near the surface of thin substrates, and this shallow-growing habit has to be respected when they are cultivated in containers.

The rhizomatous epiphytes are best handled just as their new growth phase is beginning. This ensures that the new root system produced with and from the new growth will establish rapidly in the new compost provided. The development of new growths at the base of the previous year's pseudobulb is the signal to repot. At the same time as the new growth emerges, the new roots emerge from its base. These are extremely brittle, and if damaged or bruised may then not branch readily. They should always be treated with great care, and, for ease of handling, the plants are best repotted when the new roots are less than 13 mm ($^{1}/_{2}$ in) long.

Plants should be removed carefully from their old containers, bearing in mind that much of the still-living root system tends to adhere to the wall of the pot. Always attempt to retain as much of the living root system as possible, both to assist in getting the plant off to a good start, and also to anchor it in its new pot. Carefully remove old compost from the living roots, and all dead and decayed roots. At the same time the plant can be given a general clean-up, removing old leaf sheaths and exhausted pseudobulbs. But always remember that the new growth of the orchid is to a great degree dependent upon the reserves in the pseudobulbs, and they should not be removed until they are completely spent. It is as well to err on the side of caution; if in doubt, leave the leaf-less pseudobulbs on.

The size of container chosen depends upon the

size of the plant, of its living root system, and the amount of space needed for the new growths. The rule of thumb with epiphytes is to use a pot which may appear to be a little on the small side. This is better than potting in a container which is too large, where there may be quantities of unutilised compost, which leads to problems by becoming sour and waterlogged later in the season. For this reason, epiphytes are best potted in squat or half pots, or even shallow pans. The larger surface area of the pot in relation to its volume is very helpful in ensuring the container dries rapidly. This is of importance to the maintenance of epiphytes in particular, which appreciate a wet/dry cycle in cultivation.

When potting, the rhizome of the plant should be held at a point 13 mm ($\frac{1}{2}$ in) below the level of the rim of the pot, the compost being poured in around the root system. Tap the pot a few times to ensure that the compost settles well. Neither bark- nor loam-based mixes should be firmed too greatly, or again the all-important air spaces will be lost. If the plant will not hold itself upright without assistance, it should be staked until the new roots have a firm grip.

A light watering to ensure that the compost is in close relationship with the roots may be given, but subsequent watering must be carefully watched, until the plant's new root system starts to establish (see watering, p. 35).

Potting pleiones

Pleiones, as we have already mentioned, are quite different in their growth habit from almost all other epiphytes. Whilst their growth habit may accurately be described as rhizomatous, the pseudobulbs only last for one full year, developing over the first spring and summer, flowering during the next autumn, winter or spring, and exhausting themselves completely the next growing season to produce the next growth or growths. Thus these plants are treated much more like bulbs, and can be planted in considerable numbers in pans, to create quite magnificent displays of blooms from late autumn through to the spring.

Pleiones might not require repotting each year, provided that the compost is in good condition, and we have seen superb specimen pans full of

plants, which over time will mound up upon one another. Most growers will be quite content with the displays from annually repotted pans, however, and the productivity of the plants is perhaps at its best under those conditions.

Pleiones are best repotted while completely dormant, before growth commences. They have annual root systems as well as annual pseudo-bulbs, and in order that their new roots can get a good start without disturbance and damage, most species and hybrids should be potted from December to February. Pleiones are best grown in half pots or pans, 75 mm (3 in) deep, with a few extra holes bored in the base to ensure rapid drainage.

The bulbs should be cleaned of last year's growth and dead leaf sheaths, and the dead root system trimmed to around 25 mm (1 in) long. Retaining a little of the old root system helps to keep the plants anchored when the new root system pushes out strongly after flowering, as the new growths develop. The pot should be filled with growing medium to within 25 mm (1 in) of the rim, and the pleiones placed 13–25 mm ($\frac{1}{2}$–1 in) apart. This may at first seem close, but pleiones thrive in close company, and some species will form large clumps in the wild. When the container has been filled with as many bulbs as required, fill it with growing medium to just below the rim.

Many pleione growers top-dress their plants with a layer of chopped moss (sphagnum may be used, but almost any moss will suffice), which assists in maintaining a humid microclimate around them. The plants are then kept at their normal temperatures while one awaits the flowers. They should not be watered until some signs of growth are evident.

Potting terrestrial orchids

Terrestrial orchids can be divided into two major groups, those with rhizomes and those with tubers. The approach to the cultivation of each is quite distinct. Many of the former are quite happy to spend several seasons in the same container, whilst most tuberous terrestrials have been found to respond best to being repotted annually. This does not entail completely replacing all of the compost, however, as some will be carried over from one year to the next to assist in inoculating the new compost with the orchid's mycorrhizal fungus.

Potting rhizomatous species

Two distinct groups of rhizomatous terrestrials can be distinguished, those with pseudobulbs (all of tropical affinity) and those without. The first group includes the genera *Calanthe*, *Bletilla* and *Cymbidium*. In the wild, their rhizomes tend to grow through the layers of leaf litter which overlie forest soils. In common with their epiphytic cousins, they usually grow in the upper region of a relatively thin humus layer. In cultivation, their rhizomes will eventually seek their natural level, with their pseudobulbs at or around the top of the compost.

They may spend two or three seasons in their containers, given that the condition of the potting medium is good, perhaps with a top-dressing of new compost in the spring. Repotting is best carried out just as growth recommences, either because the plant has outgrown the container or because of the condition of the compost. This allows for the new root system to establish itself in the new medium immediately.

With very open media such as we recommend, extra drainage material is not required for plants which will spend only one year in a pot. However, if plants are left for two or more seasons, a layer of chippings or charcoal at the base of the pot may be of benefit in retaining sharp drainage and 'sweet' conditions throughout. Again, as with all the other orchids we are dealing with, broad-based squat pots, half pots or pans are recommended.

The pot should be filled to about 75 mm (3 in) from the top with compost, remembering to carry over around 20 per cent of the old compost from the previous pot. Firm lightly, and place the orchid plant at its final growing height. The rhizome should lie about 13–25 mm ($^1/_2$–1 in) below the final level of the compost. The pseudo-bulbs will be near or at the surface of the compost; in the case of *Calanthe* perhaps just emerging through it. Finish filling the pot to within 13 mm ($^1/_2$ in) of the rim, and then firm lightly, prior to watering in.

Unlike their tropical epiphytic counterparts, the terrestrials appreciate some readily available moisture from the time they are repotted onwards. Other pseudobulbous terrestrial genera which may be treated this way include *Liparis*, *Cremastra* and *Malaxis*.

Other rhizomatous terrestrials

Two further groups of rhizomatous terrestrials must be considered. The deciduous types, including genera such as *Cypripedium*, *Epipactis* and *Cephalanthera*, possess rather slender rhizomes, which are still of great importance in providing reserves of nourishment to the new shoots as they emerge in spring. The other group contains the evergreen *Goodyera* species, northern outliers of a group of tropical forest floor species, with fleshy rhizomes and leaves which may be attractively marked.

Conventional wisdom suggests that all of these should be treated in much the same way as most other orchids, i.e. potting around the time that growth recommences after dormancy. Recent work in the USA by Whitlow (1983), with *Cypripedium* in particular, has suggested that equally good, if not better, results, can be obtained by handling the plants in the autumn. This is particularly important if one wishes to propagate them, as the crucial food reserves are then more evenly distributed throughout the rhizome. In spring, with new growth underway, those reserves move towards the leading shoot, and small back portions cannot call upon good reserves for establishment.

He argues also that the habit of cypripediums especially, with their large and very soft growth buds produced rapidly in the spring, might lead to inadvertent damage to new growths during handling, and consequent failure to establish well. His methods certainly deserve consideration, when his results with autumn repotting and division are considered. In keeping with general practice, he recommends repotting no more frequently than every two, or preferably three, years.

Using Whitlow's method, the plants are handled as the leaves fall. It may well be that the roots can then re-establish to some degree, with the residual warmth of the season. Whether potted

Figure 7
Potting cycle for rhizomatous species:
A, ingredients:
a, powdered lime,
b, bonemeal, **c**, fresh compost, **d**, old compost;
B, cross-section of pot, showing position of rhizome;
C, view of pot, plant and label

in autumn or spring, the plants can be handled as their pseudobulbous counterparts are. The container is filled to within 75 mm (3 in) of the top, remembering to take over 20–30 per cent of the compost from the previous container. Whitlow grows his cypripediums in boxes for preference, between 300–450 mm (12–18 in) square, and up to 300 mm (12 in) deep.

The plants are placed with their roots spread over the surface of the mix, and the container is then filled, and lightly firmed. The tip of the leading growth bud should be just level with the top of the compost when the pot is filled to within 13 mm (½ in) of the rim. Many growers find that a top-dressing of a mixture of leafmould and/or grit and chippings is of benefit. This ensures that the surface of the mix will not 'cap', so that water and air can pass in (and out) easily, and it also suppresses the growth of mosses and liverworts. The top-dressing can be replaced annually. After potting, a light watering to settle in the soil is necessary; subsequently the compost should be kept moist, rather than wet, over the dormant period.

This method is also suitable for other rhizomatous terrestrials, such as *Epipactis* and *Cephalanthera*. The final potting level may vary from species to species; but if one begins by using the above system, it can be varied in subsequent years according to how the plants react.

Potting Goodyera

This small but choice group of evergreen species are typically found in shady forest floor habitats. They can grow as leaf litter terrestrials, or crawling over moist, moss-covered rocks and tree stumps. Shallow pans are certainly preferable for this group, whose roots do not delve deep into their containers. They are best handled in spring, potting into a very open mix. The woodland terrestrial mix D (see page 27), with extra leaf-mould worked into the top surface, will suit most species well. They may also be persuaded to grow over and on mossy rocks or branches, or on peat blocks set into pots, to provide fascinating little landscapes in miniature. The miniature *Cypripedium debile* has also recently been successfully grown in this manner.

In the Far East growers of terrestrial species will occasionally go to great lengths to mimic the ecology of the plants they grow. At the 12th World Orchid Conference in Tokyo, Japan, the authors saw *Ponerorchis* being grown in a hole in a small branch, filled with leafy soil, to mimic how the plant had been found growing in the wild.

Whilst such methods of cultivation are related to the cultural appreciation that local growers have for reproducing nature, they are nevertheless soundly based on the principles we have discussed, and have been used with success for many years.

Potting tuberous terrestrials

We have already discussed how the tuberous species, contrary to popular belief, actually do better when repotted on an annual basis. There are of course orchid species, such as the colony-forming *Serapias* and *Pterostylis*, which will do well for two or three years in the same container. Problems, however, can arise, particularly if the compost deteriorates, and disease sets in. It also appears that the annual repotting technique is of particular benefit to the many genera which until recently were considered intractable in cultivation.

The reason might well lie in the way this technique greatly mimics natural conditions. In the wild, the growth of these plants depends on and benefits from an infusion of fresh organic matter on an annual cycle, as the surrounding vegetation dies down and becomes a food source for saprophytic fungi in the soil. Orchid mycorrhizae, as a part of this system, will obviously benefit from fresh organic matter — both in the wild, and in cultivation in pots. The desire to maintain ideal soil structure in the container, and to replenish the organic matter on a regular basis, lead inexorably to the necessity to repot annually.

The containers chosen for growing mature terrestrials should not be too small. A single plant of a small-growing *Ophrys* species may be accommodated in a 100 mm (4 in) pot, but for optimal results we would suggest growing terrestrial orchids in groups, of perhaps three to five, in larger containers (125–150 mm (5–6 in) at least). Up to ten (or with smaller *Pterostylis* many more) plants of the true colony-formers can be comfortably accommodated in such a container. Larger-growing species, for example certain dactylorhizas, may require a 200–250 mm (8–10 in) pot to accommodate several plants comfortably. Obviously, the management of small orchid plants with relatively small root systems, in such large containers is rather different from that of most other commonly cultivated plants. To provide ideal conditions for both orchid and fungus, the management of the compost is of paramount importance.

The non-colony-forming species, the great majority of tuberous terrestrials, unfortunately do not as a rule increase rapidly in cultivation. Genera such as *Ophrys* and *Orchis* fall into this group. Many species will multiply vegetatively only slowly (unless encouraged — see Propagation, p. 41).

The best time to repot these orchids is during their dormancy. No danger then exists of inadvertent damage to newly emerging shoots and roots. Broadly speaking, the dormancy of most Mediterranean species occurs during summer, with the first signs of growth evident from around August onwards, depending on the season and the way the plants are treated. Australasian terrestrials are also for the most part summer dormant. Some species from high altitudes, or the farthest south localities (Tasmania and southern New

Zealand, for example), may tend towards a winter cold season dormancy.

Northern European and high altitude south European species are for the most part winter dormant (with exceptions in 'southern' genera such as *Ophrys* and *Orchis.*

The evergreen *Disa* species are an exception to the general rules regarding terrestrial orchids, as under ideal conditions most have no true dormant period. New growths arise from their tubers as the old rosette dies off during the summer. They can safely be repotted after the flowers have faded, or as the old rosette shows signs of dying off.

If southern hemisphere plants are newly imported, it will take one or two seasons to turn them around to the correct seasonality. But after this one should be led by what the plants wish to do. If they prefer to grow in the autumn, there is little that can be done to prevent this, and they will have to be given adequate protection to maintain them through their preferred growing season. A well-selected collection of terrestrial orchids in a cool greenhouse can ensure the bonus of flowers for most of the year.

Prior to repotting, the first instruction should be 'first catch your hare!', advice that may at first seem rather obvious. However, it can be difficult to find some small orchid tubers, especially in the colony-formers such as the smaller *Pterostylis* and *Serapias*, which reproduce quite freely. *Corybas* is a particular problem in this respect. Often the smaller tubers will be only as large as a small piece of grit. We recommend that the entire contents of the pot be passed through a 5 mm ($^1/_4$ in) sieve, the contents of which can then be checked for tubers. Those who have eyesight problems should avail themselves of a ×10 lens to ensure they don't miss anything! Some growers of our acquaintance actually retain all the potting mix in which the 'problem' species have been grown, to ensure that none gets away.

Like many bulbs, most of the tuberous terrestrial orchids (disas excepted) have annual root systems. Unlike bulbs, the new roots of orchids emerge from immediately below the dormant bud, and not the base of the tuber. Thus they must be planted sufficiently deep to ensure that the roots are well covered with compost.

Many terrestrial orchid growers place a barrier to pests such as woodlice at the bottom of the pot. A piece of coarse woven shade mesh should suffice. As well as keeping pests out, this also prevents the problem with many terrestrial orchids which have 'droppers', i.e. tubers that naturally seek out the bottom of the pot, and can either root into benches and be damaged or lost, or otherwise may fall prey to wandering pests.

With the barrier in place, the pot should be filled with compost to 50 mm (2 in) below the rim, and lightly firmed. The tubers should be planted in this layer, with the top of the dormant buds level with the compost. These will then be around 37 mm ($1^1/_2$ in) below the final surface of the compost. The pot can then be filled to within 13 mm ($^1/_2$ in) of the surface. Some growers like to fill to a slightly lower level, and then top-dress with gritty sand. Australian growers use locally available organic mulches, such as *Casuarina* needles. Top-dressing is optional, given an ideal very open free-draining mix, but if you find your compost tends to harden and 'cap' at the surface, or that mosses and liverworts become a problem, certainly top-dressing will alleviate this, and subsequent difficulties with watering and aeration of the compost.

Tubers should be planted so that when they grow the plants are not overcrowded. A little space is needed around each plant, to enable irrigation without allowing water to lie for prolonged periods in the growths. This can be dangerous, especially for winter growers, with rot diseases a constant problem. Smaller-growing non-colony-formers, the majority of species, should have three to five plants in a 125–150 mm (5–6 in) pot. Larger-growing species will need a larger container. Colony-formers such as *Pterostylis* and *Corybas* may be planted between 13–25 mm ($^1/_2$–1 in) apart. A well filled, but not overfull, pot of the latter is a pleasing thing to see. If in doubt, always go to a larger, or extra, container. It may well be the plants will be more productive without excessive competition.

Disas should always be potted very softly indeed. The structure of their open peat and perlite composts will be badly affected by excessive firming.

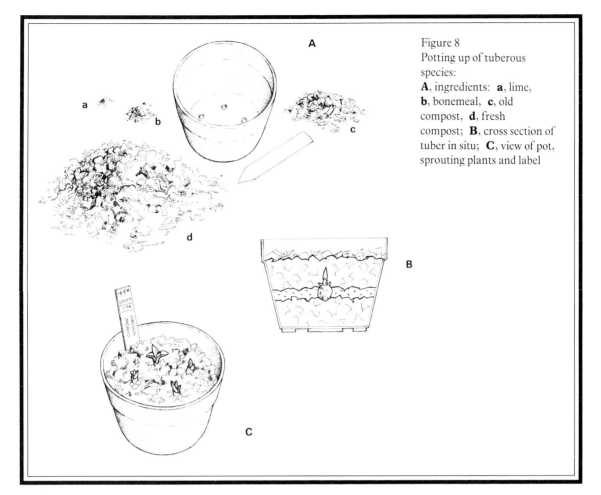

Figure 8
Potting up of tuberous species:
A, ingredients: **a**, lime, **b**, bonemeal, **c**, old compost, **d**, fresh compost; **B**, cross section of tuber in situ; **C**, view of pot, sprouting plants and label

After potting, lightly water to settle the compost in the container, and then continue with the watering regime as required for the time of year and stage of growth of the plants (see watering, below).

WATERING AND FEEDING

The daily and seasonal cultural regimes of a mixed collection of terrestrial orchids vary according to their provenance, and thus the season when they are in growth. However, certain basic rules apply to almost all the plants one may grow. Exceptions will be noted as necessary.

Watering

Different watering regimes are required for the three major divisions of hardy orchids: the epiphytic species; rhizomatous terrestrials and tuberous species from more northerly areas or alpine habitats; and species from Mediterranean climates, whether of the northern or southern hemispheres.

Water quality

Water quality is of some importance to orchid cultivation. This applies not only to the pH of the water, but also to the amount of dissolved salts in it. Water of a neutral to slightly acidic pH (6.5–7.0) is best. Rain water is almost perfect, given that it is stored correctly, although in some areas excess acidity may be a problem (say much below a pH of 5). This is easily checked with home pH testing kits. Slightly alkaline water (up to about pH 7.5–7.8) should present no problems with the relatively short pot-life of many terrestrial orchids, which begin in an acid to neutral compost. If water has to be softened for use with orchids, water softeners which exchange calcium and magnesium for sodium should never be used, as sodium is far more dangerous to orchids.

Water with a naturally high concentration of dissolved salts, especially sodium, can lead to problems with orchids. Fortunately, this is uncommon in most areas where hardy orchids can be grown. Other salts will bind to the clay fraction in a loam-based mix, and thus be rendered harmless for the pot-life of most terrestrials, when they are repotted annually.

Watering epiphytes

Whatever conditions they grow under in their natural habitats, most epiphytes appreciate a definite wet/dry cycle in cultivation. Their open composts (especially those based upon bark chippings) tend to dry quite rapidly when fresh, but become more retentive as they age. By that time the plants should have established a root system causing the compost to dry more rapidly. Tropical orchid growers usually allow their plants to become quite dry before watering (which can easily be tested by lifting the pot, as epiphyte composts are very light when dry). They must then be watered thoroughly, until the water runs freely from the drainage holes in the pot.

All of the epiphytes which might be accommodated in a hardy orchid collection will be vegetatively dormant in the winter, and their water requirement drops away dramatically, especially under the low temperatures which prevail. Keeping the plants too wet will almost certainly lead to loss of their roots. The pots should only be watered when dry, and then only lightly. Some species may show a definite wrinkling of the pseudobulbs during their dormancy. This is nothing to be concerned about, unless they appear to be wasting away completely, when a light watering should help to restore them.

One genus in particular requires no water at all during its dormancy. *Pleione*, with its deciduous habit and annual root system, must remain completely dry until leaf growth recommences in the spring.

When growth begins plants should be watered more frequently. Newly repotted plants will need careful attention to avoid problems with the compost, which can be excessively dry if under-watered, or may become sodden if over-watered. The state of the compost should dictate watering as and when the pot feels substantially lighter. During the main growing season the pots may be kept moister, but a definite drying should be allowed before watering. *Pleione* is again an exception to this rule, and when in full growth will prefer to be kept moister than most other epiphytes. A panful of pleiones contains rather more plants than normally accommodated in a container, and will accordingly dry out more rapidly.

The initial watering of pleiones as they start to grow is also a little more tricky. As the new leaves and flowers are produced, so new roots will push strongly from the base of the growths. The pots will require a thorough watering at this stage, to ensure that there is moisture for the roots to seek out at the bottom of the pot. The next watering may not be necessary for two weeks or so, but as the growths develop so watering can be increased in frequency. By the time the leaves are fully developed, the full summer watering regime will be required, and the pots should not be allowed to become as dry as will other epiphytes.

Towards the end of the season, when the growths of epiphytic species have been fully made up, and temperatures are falling away, watering can be gradually reduced, until the winter state is reached. This assists in ripening the growths, in readiness for flowering the following season. The signal to stop watering pleiones is given as the leaves yellow and fall.

All of the rules above are designed for plants growing in a bark-based epiphyte mix, but they are just as appropriate for plants in loam-based composts. However, loam-based mixes, with their much more retentive nature, require particular care in watering as the compost does not dry so rapidly.

Watering terrestrials

Terrestrial orchids appreciate a more even moisture regime whilst in growth, although they may require a wet/dry cycle seasonally. They divide into two main groups: those from seasonally dry Mediterranean climates which need to be dried off for their dormancy; and those from high altitudes, or higher latitudes, which have a cold moist dormancy, and need to be kept somewhat wetter. The evergreen *Disa* species and hybrids do not have any dormant period as such, and appreciate moist conditions throughout the year.

Dry season terrestrials

This group includes the southern European and Australian species. On an annual cycle, they will be lightly watered immediately after repotting, to settle the compost and provide a little background moisture for their new roots. If the new compost is allowed to become completely dry in the pot, re-wetting may be a problem. As new growth commences, the pots should be watered more frequently, until they are being kept moist, but not wet. There must always be space in the medium for air. This watering regime usually begins in about August, depending on the seasonality of the plants being dealt with.

Towards the end of the season, after the flowers have faded, and as the rosettes begin to die off, watering is reduced until it almost ceases. However, it must not stop completely, as plants being grown in containers can become excessively desiccated during the summer, when they are best left in a shady, reasonably humid place (conditions in the alpine house suit them admirably). Water should still be given, about every three–four weeks, to maintain some moisture in the pot, and keep the tubers plump. In this condition, they are better set to grow away strongly at the proper time.

Cold season terrestrials

The basics of watering are exactly as with their dry season counterparts, with one major difference in that they require more definitely moist conditions during their dormancy. Again, moist, but not wet or sodden, conditions are sought at the roots.

Plants which have cold season dormancies include most of those from moist or boggy habitats, and those from tropical regions. Special attention should be paid to ensure that they are kept properly moist throughout the growing season, as they will not tolerate occasional dry conditions as well as the dry season terrestrials.

Feeding and fertilisers

Most orchids are particularly adapted to grow in poor soils; in cultivation, this adaptation may manifest itself as an intolerance of excessively generous feeding regimes. To put figures to this, many orchids are grown commercially with fertiliser concentrations in water of around 300–1,000 parts per million, while other crops, such as tomatoes, may well demand 4,000–5,000 ppm. The key to a successful fertiliser regime with orchids is 'little and often'. Feeding regularly with low concentrations of fertiliser provides the regular injection of background nutrients that orchids appear to appreciate.

Feeding epiphytic orchids

As with so many other aspects of orchid culture, there are two distinct approaches to feeding orchid plants. Again, the main dichotomy is between the tropical epiphytes, and the terrestrials being grown 'symbiotically'. The former can be fed in the same way as other tropical orchids, using a weak balanced fertiliser, with equal proportions of nitrogen, potassium and phosphate, regularly during the growing season. Special orchid fertilisers may be used, or other formulations designed for houseplants, at reduced strength (about quarter to half that recommended). Inorganic fertilisers are perfectly appropriate for epiphytes.

The terrestrial disas from South Africa, growing in peat and perlite composts, may be fed as epiphytes are. They will also benefit from foliar feeding during the winter, as do the terrestrials (see below). All rhizomatous terrestrials in epiphyte mixes should also be fed as epiphytes.

To prevent any build-up of salts in the compost, which can harm the sensitive roots of the plants, regular flushings of water alone are recommended. During the summer, say from May to September, plants may be fed at two out of every three waterings. Outside of this season, they may be fed at alternate waterings. From November to March no pot feeding at all should be given.

Feeding terrestrial orchids

There is a genuine difference of opinion as to feeding regimes for orchids being grown with the benefit of mycorrhizal symbionts. Most authorities appear to agree that, in all but a few special cases, for example the growing of wetland orchids in artificial sphagnum bogs, some form of base-dressing of fertiliser is of benefit. This will usually be organic in nature, as we have already discussed in the section on composts. But beyond that, supplying extra nutrients in artificial form during the growth of the plants is not recommended by a number of growers.

Experience at Kew leads the authors to the conclusion that there is little to lose, and may be much to gain, from supplementing the diet of orchids being grown symbiotically with occasional feeds. In order to ensure that this will not interfere with the growth of the fungal symbionts, this feeding can be given through the foliage. Occasional weak balanced foliar feeds (with equal proportions of nitrogen to potassium and phosphate), may be given throughout the period of growth, at a quarter of the recommended strength for other plants.

The frequency of feeding depends upon the subject and the time of year. Winter-growing orchids may be fed fortnightly during the shorter days (say from October to March), increasing the rate to weekly in April, until growth ceases. Summer growers may be fed weekly from the time their leaves are fully developed, until they begin to fade and fall.

Such a feeding regime has not been found to cause any direct harm, and the overall health of the terrestrial orchids grown under it can only lead to the conclusion it has been of some direct benefit. It must always be remembered that gardeners seek the maximum productivity from their charges, and that they do many things that are not necessarily crucial to the survival of their plants, but which are none the less of benefit.

PESTS AND DISEASES

Most orchid ailments and their controls are common to all other ornamental plants. The old advice, that one should always seek to nip problems in the bud, by keeping a good eye on the plants for any tell-tale signs, should be followed. The key to a healthy orchid collection lies essentially in obtaining good healthy stock, in good cultivation practices, and in prompt diagnosis and control of pests and diseases.

Pests

Pests can be divided into two major categories; the biting and chewing, i.e. slugs, snails, weevils, etc.; and the suckers, including aphids, mealy bugs, scale insects and mites. The chemical controls we recommend are safe to use on orchids, as long as the manufacturers' instructions are strictly followed. Active ingredients have been listed wherever possible, rather than brand names which may vary from time to time, and country to country.

Before we move on to describe the various orchid ailments, the final point to be made is that, for safety of both the grower and the plants, all spraying and other operations must be carried out in accordance with instructions on the label. Avoid spraying when the plants are under stress, particularly in hot sunny weather. Bright (but not sunny), buoyant conditions are best, to avoid problems with damage to plants and flowers from chemicals.

Sucking pests

Aphids are a particular problem with the soft growths and inflorescences of orchids. They may be active very early in the year, even in a cold greenhouse. They are implicated in the spread of virus conditions, which can be very damaging to orchids, and should be controlled, when first seen. Control: derris, pyrethroids, malathion, gamma HCH, dimethoate.

Mealy bugs tend to be more of a problem with the warmer-growing orchids, evergreens in particular, as they require somewhere to spend the cold season. They can show up in cold houses as well, but as yet we have not found them a problem on deciduous terrestrials. They are mobile, covered in a white mealy wax, and tend to hide away in the centre of growths. Control: diazinon, malathion, dimethoate, deltamethrin — all with a wetting agent to increase effectiveness.

Scale insects: Again, this pest is more of a problem with warmer-growing evergreen species. Scales on orchids may be soft bodied or hard, and whitish, brown or black in colour. Some species concentrate in leaf sheaths; with others, the young migrate to the soft parts of plants. Control: immature stages by using malathion, diazinon and deltamethrin; adults by malathion, dimethoate and carbaryl.

Whitefly: Whilst not a pest of epiphytic orchids, glasshouse whitefly can be a problem on disas and terrestrials, especially late in the season of growth of the winter-growing species. Control: smokes of propoxior or gamma HCH.

All the above pests secrete honeydew, on which black sooty mould may grow, this is often one of the first overt signs of infestation, especially with pests that hide away amongst the foliage.

Red spider mites: These can be a considerable nuisance on thin-leafed orchids, in which group many of the terrestrials fall. They are very small, just visible to the naked eye, and their first damage to foliage is a fine stippling on the underside, where they feed. Severe infestations will lead to the production of silvery webbing all over the plants, and feeding on all the plant surfaces. They are a particular problem if relative humidities fall below the optimal, and thrive in bright dry conditions. Control: derris, dicofol, dimethoate. Reproduction is stopped by using dienochlor (marketed as Pentac).

Chewing and biting pests

Slugs and snails: Especially found in damp and humid conditions, leaving tell-tale slime trails.

Control: baits, powders or drenches of metaldehyde of methiocarb. Symbiotically grown terrestrials should not be drenched.

Cockroaches: Nocturnal in habit, preferring to attack young shoots, flowers or root tips. Control: gamma HCH, permethrin, deltamethrin (these controls also apply to other beetles).

Thrips: Small black insects which may cause fine silvery stippling on the upper sides of foliage. Control: malathion, gamma HCH, diazinon, dimethoate.

Fungus gnats: Small flying insects, whose larvae will attack very soft seedlings and break down composts based on peat. Control: gamma HCH, pyrethrum-based insecticides.

Weevils: May attack leaves causing semi-circular holes in the edges (vine weevils). Their larvae may also attack tubers in the soil. Control: gamma HCH.

Other pests

Worms: More of nuisance value, their activities can ruin the structure of the compost in a pot. They can be flushed out by a watering with pyrethrum, at the usual rate for control of aphids.

Mice: May attack tubers, which are high in starch, and young growths. Control with traps and baits.

Eelworms: This destructive pest has recently been reported upon dactylorhizas grown commercially. Infected plants may show pale streaking and flecking of leaves, some distortion of the roots and tubers, and a general tendency not to thrive. There is no effective control available to amateurs. Care should be taken only to obtain healthy stock, rejecting plants which have unexplained symptoms that cause concern. If eelworm is diagnosed, infected plants should be discarded, and the compost or soil in which they were growing either discarded or sterilised. Eelworms may spread along sand benches in the moisture present around the base of the pots. Growing upon slatted staging will help to prevent this.

Diseases

The chief problems which may occur are caused by fungi and bacteria, although viruses are potentially very damaging to orchids, but their control is very much based on cultural routines.

Virus diseases

The most likely group of plants to be infected with viruses are the epiphytes, or genera such as *Dactylorhiza*, with a long history of cultivation being propagated mainly by vegetative means. Many plants in general cultivation have been infected by gardeners handling them, cutting into their tissues, etc., without due care and attention. The chief symptoms of virus diseases are colourless or black streaking of leaves (chlorotic or necrotic respectively), although the leaf symptoms. may be in oval or circular patterns also. Growth of infected plants may be generally poor, and when they flower, the blooms may well be distorted or show numerous small brown necrotic patches.

There are no controls, infected plants should be discarded. The main agent of spread is undoubtedly the grower, who by using the same tools to cut into the tissue of a number of plants without sterilising them spreads infection in sap from plant to plant. All cutting tools used on orchids should be sterilised with a propane torch, or by soaking in 10 per cent trisodium orthophosphate.

Bacterial rots

These may occur spontaneously, perhaps effecting entry through damage by pests. Soft brown areas of tissue, accompanied sometimes by an offensive smell, are the first signs. Soft foliage in particular is likely to be attacked. Control is to some degree by cultural means, cutting off all affected tissue, avoiding close stagnant conditions (plenty of air movement and proper humidity levels), and not allowing water to lodge in growths overnight or during cold weather. Bactericides such as quaternary ammonium compound (marketed as Physan) will assist in stopping the spread of the disease, as will drying off the plants for a while, or placing them in a strong airstream, such as immediately in front of or beneath a fan. With the epiphytes,

bacterial rot problems may be alleviated by giving two feeds with commercial high-potash fertilisers towards the end of the growing season, to assist in ripening growths.

Fungal diseases

These divide into two major types, the rots, and the 'dry' symptom conditions, such as rusts.

Rots are often prevalent in still, dank conditions. Leaf, stem, rhizome and tuber rots are often characterised by a purple stain produced in the leading edge of the infected area. Control by cutting off all infected areas of tissue, and spraying or dipping the plant in Physan. Root rots are usually associated with poor aeration and drainage in the potting medium. Affected plants should be repotted immediately, with all affected tissue being cut off and discarded. Epiphytes may be treated with a broad spectrum fungicide such as benomyl. The same recourse may be necessary with terrestrials should the rescue of a badly infected plant be the aim. Control of fungal conditions of symbiotically grown terrestrials is best effected by sprays of the (usually above-ground) infected parts with non-systemic fungicides such as Physan. But occasionally, to attempt to save the plant in question, systemic remedies are essential.

Tuberous terrestrials in particular are attacked by a systemic fungal condition, which may show in the foliage as black streaking and spotting of the leaves, moving back into the stem and tuber. Once in the stem of the rosette, the death of the plant often follows, and certainly the above ground parts have to be cut off in order to save the tuber. In our experience this condition has been more prevalent when plants have been grown in pots placed directly on sand or gravel, leading us to surmise that it may be waterborne, and more likely to show up when plants root through into benches, with subsequent damage should they be moved.

Rusts: Rust fungi, characterised by the production of orange-red pustules of spores on foliage and stems, may be a problem with terrestrial orchids, being far less prevalent on epiphytes. Control by destroying affected parts, and spraying generally with ferbam or zineb as a preventative. Other leafspot fungi may attack a wide range of orchids, with unsightly, but not fatal results. Small sunken spots, perhaps with a purple-black line around the edge, may enlarge and coalesce. Control with sprays of zineb or ferbam. Leaf dieback from the tips, which may have a number of cultural or fungal causes, will (if caused by fungi) be controlled by copper preparations, zineb or benomyl.

Cultural problems that lead to leaf tip dieback are mainly caused by lack of trace elements, and can be remedied by ensuring the plants have these as part of their normal feeding regime. They are more prevalent with epiphytes growing in bark-based mixes.

Moulds: Grey mould (*Botrytis*) will usually be found on dead tissue, but can spread to living parts in dank conditions. Under cold, humid conditions, the germination of botrytis spores on flowers can also cause brown spotting, especially with tropical epiphytes. Initial prevention and control is by ensuring good air movement, refraining from spraying over the plants in very dull humid weather, and only spraying over first thing in the day otherwise. For leaf and stem infections, cut off affected parts, spray with benomyl, and dust all cut surfaces with sulphur to prevent re-infection. Flower infections should be cured by cultural means.

PROPAGATION

With a few notable exceptions, orchids tend to increase relatively slowly in cultivation. This is particularly true of many tuberous terrestrials, which unless encouraged, will go for year after year producing a replacement tuber but no more. Propagation of orchids from seed requires quite sophisticated techniques and equipment. Epiphytic species are quite straightforward by comparison with the majority of the terrestrials. The age-old technique of sowing seed around a 'mother plant', in order to take advantage of the symbiotic fungus which is associated with it, can occasionally produce results, but that is a relatively haphazard method.

As with so many other aspects of orchid cultivation, the tuberous species require quite different techniques from those with rhizomes.

Propagating rhizomatous orchids

Orchids may be divided in the same way as any other rhizomatous herbaceous perennial. An important point to bear in mind is that divisions should not, as a rule, be too small. Orchids have their reserves in the older growths or rhizome, and these are mobilised and moved forward to the leading shoot; so for best establishment of the new division, it is important that there be sufficient reserves present. For pseudobulbous orchids, this usually means the leading growth, and a section of rhizome with at least two (preferably three) pseudobulbs. The same rule can be applied to rhizomatous species without pseudobulbs, dividing according to the past growths, which can be seen as joints along the rhizome. Again, for preference, three growth divisions are best.

The accepted wisdom with rhizomatous orchids has always been to propagate early in the growing season. This certainly applies with the pseudobulbous species, with better establishment secured at that time. If plants are prepared for division during the previous growing season, growers can obtain the bonus of stimulating back divisions into producing new growths. Plants are prepared for this by cutting half-way through the rhizome at the point where you wish to divide. Cutting off the supply of hormones from the leading growth, which otherwise suppresses the growth of dormant eyes, will lead to the development of growth buds at the point of division. Back divisions can always be taken without this preparation, but establishment will be nothing like as rapid or certain. This method, usually used with epiphytic species, has also been successfully employed for *Cypripedium*.

Pleione is a major exception to the general rules of propagation. Pleiones transfer all the reserves of the previous year's pseudobulb into the current year's, and thus never develop a proper rhizome. Under good conditions most species and hybrids will give two growths and bulbs from the initial one, but as an added bonus some will also produce

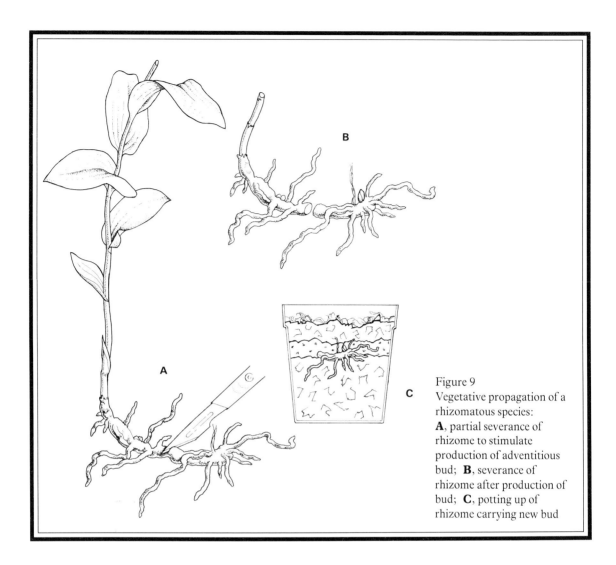

Figure 9
Vegetative propagation of a rhizomatous species:
A, partial severance of rhizome to stimulate production of adventitious bud; **B**, severance of rhizome after production of bud; **C**, potting up of rhizome carrying new bud

plantlets around the rim of the pseudobulb. In most cases these are large enough to remove and grow on in a somewhat finer mixture than required for the adult plants. (Details are given in Cribb and Butterfield (1988)). *Pleione humilis*, however, tends to have very small bulbils, which will need to be started into growth on a bed of moss, to provide the close humid conditions such small plants appreciate. Even under those conditions, considerable losses will occur with bulbils which can be as small as lettuce seed.

Propagation of Cypripedium

Work by Whitlow (1983) in the USA, and by Dryden in England, suggests that this genus, and perhaps other non-pseudobulbous rhizomatous terrestrials, are best divided towards the end of the growing season. At this time, the reserves of starch that the plant has been building up all season are distributed fairly evenly throughout the rhizome. Small divisions of a lead and two growths, and back divisions without any developed leading bud, have been found to establish very well using this technique. As a bonus, the likelihood of damage occurring to soft new growths in the spring is greatly reduced. The residual heat in the soil or compost at this time will assist the roots in re-establishing themselves prior to the dormant season.

Propagation of tuberous terrestrials

Tuberous terrestrials show considerable variation in their willingness to reproduce themselves vegetatively. Genera such as *Pterostylis* have species which are vigorous colony-formers, others break new growths only rarely. Amongst the European species, *Ophrys* is characterised by only rarely forming new offsets, whereas *Serapias* falls at the other end of the spectrum, and readily forms colonies.

The South African disas differ slightly in their propensity to propagate themselves, having both replacement tubers, and stolons which will form extra rosettes, developing tubers in due course. We will deal with those separately.

The main replacement growth of tuberous terrestrials develops immediately below the rosette, and is usually fully mature by the time that flowering takes place. It is this habit of growth that gives the opportunity to coax the plants into producing extra tubers, essentially by the expedient of removing the new tuber. The shock of this, and the removal of any hormonal influence which it may exert to prevent the growth of any other dormant eyes into tubers, is an effective means of propagation.

The two major methods can broadly be described as 'summer' and 'winter' propagation. As they have been developed principally with European species, they take their seasonal names from the growth habit of the majority of plants from that area. But they are equally appropriate for terrestrials from other parts of the world, at the same stages of growth, at whatever time of year that may be.

Summer propagation

This method is used just as the flowers begin to fade (which may be any time from early spring onwards, depending on the plants being grown, and the conditions under which they are housed). Remove the plant from its pot, and separate the new tuber from the rosette by cutting the stolon, or at the place of attachment. The rosette and old tuber, which should have most of the root system

intact, should then be repotted in the normal way, as should the new tuber.

Aftercare of the two differs. The new tuber should immediately be treated as if dormant, whilst the flowered shoot and old tuber should be kept in growth for as long as possible, to allow the maximum opportunity for new tubers to develop before dormancy. Do not allow seed set, or the rosette will die off more rapidly, and reserves will be taken from tuber production to seed production. Shady, moist conditions will delay dormancy in those species which are summer, or dry season resters. After the rosette has died down, give the normal conditions for rest, and thereafter treat normally.

Winter propagation

This method, recently described by Ingrid Von Ramin (1976) of the Palmengarten in Frankfurt, uses the unflowered rosette at the stage of growth that winter-growing species reach around mid-December in the northern hemisphere. By this time, many species will have a fully developed rosette, with a developing replacement tuber.

The entire new growth is removed from the old tuber from which it has arisen, the cut being made towards the bottom of the stem, leaving a small portion with one or two roots still attached to the old tuber. As both pieces will be grown on as normally the operation may be performed without the plant being removed from its pot. If this is difficult to achieve in practice, the plant may be removed from its pot, and the two pieces then grown on separately. The original rosette should flower as normal, and produce a replacement tuber, whilst the old tuber should develop one or maybe two new growths from dormant axillary buds on the small piece of stem left when the rosette was removed, with new tubers.

Normal growing conditions, and normal dormancy, can be given to all plants treated this way. At whatever time of year tuberous terrestrials may reach the stage of growth outlined above, they may be propagated as described.

Vegetative propagation of Disa

Disas are tuberous terrestrials, although they have the ability to propagate themselves by stolons

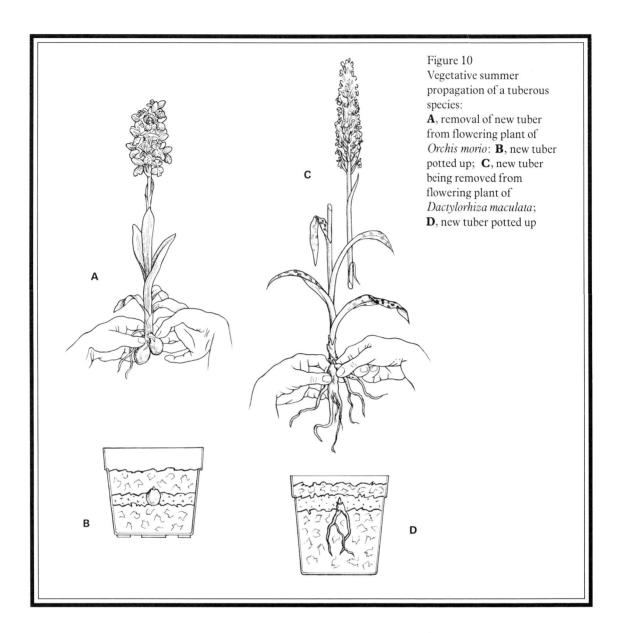

Figure 10
Vegetative summer propagation of a tuberous species:
A, removal of new tuber from flowering plant of *Orchis morio*: **B**, new tuber potted up; **C**, new tuber being removed from flowering plant of *Dactylorhiza maculata*; **D**, new tuber potted up

which produce new rosettes, under which tubers will develop in time. These stolons may grow down to the base of the pot, and the new rosettes appear through the drainage holes. Disas flower in the late spring and early summer, and should be propagated after flowering. As the old flower stem dies down, the new shoot on the replacement tuber will usually have started into growth, and the tuber can be removed and repotted as normally. If the old flower stem has sufficient reserves, new axillary growths may appear from the leaves at its base. Keep the old rosette should this appear to be happening. The small growths produced in this way will grow away and can be potted separately during their second year of growth. Rosettes may be found to be arising from stolons, and these can be potted separately if they are well developed and possess an independent root system. When well grown, disas increase quite readily in cultivation.

Raising orchids from seed

The 'natural' method

The key to this method is to use the mycorrhizal fungus, present in the pot, to germinate seed sown around the 'mother' plant. Given the quite slow rate of development of orchid seedlings, this method requires that the mother plant be undisturbed for at least an entire season after sowing the seed around it, or any tiny seedlings may effectively be lost in the repotting process. Should there by any seedlings in the pot in the season immediately following sowing, great care must be taken to ensure that they are not lost sight of by the time the plants come to be repotted. It may be as well for the first few seasons of growth to keep the offspring with the mother plant. Once they have developed to a size from which they can safely be grown on, large enough to keep track of, they may be treated exactly as mature plants.

Disas once again are quite different in their requirements. They have comparatively large seed, and can be propagated readily by sowing on to a medium of sphagnum moss, or sphagnum moss peat, and then being raised much as one would fern spores. They require initial conditions of high humidity to germinate, and subsequently must be kept continually moist.

Disa seed pods take from around one to three months to mature, and should be removed just as the stem attaching them to the spike begins to yellow, before the pod splits. Keep the pod in a sealed packet, in a refrigerator at between 3–5°C (37–41°F), until the seed is to be sown. Seed can be sown on to sphagnum moss which has been boiled for five minutes. The moss is squeezed to remove excess water, and placed in a clean container, firming lightly. Sow the seed evenly on the surface, and cover it with a piece of glass. A temperature of around 12–20°C (55–70°F), and a shady position, are required for germination. Medium-grade sphagnum moss peat may also be used as the sowing medium.

Place the container in a saucer of water with a low pH (preferably between 5–5.5), and allow the water to be taken up by capillary action, rather than watering from above. The moss or peat medium should never be allowed to dry out. Seed should take around four weeks to germinate. As the seedlings develop they may gradually be exposed to air by slightly raising the glass, until they are in ambient conditions. Prick out and grow on when plants are large enough to handle safely.

In vitro culture of orchid seedlings

Commercially important orchids, principally in tropical epiphytic genera, have been raised from seed in sterile conditions *in vitro* (literal translation, in glass), for many years. Using this technique, growers are able to bypass the obligate requirement of orchids for a fungal symbiont in order to germinate and establish in the wild. Seed is sown on to an agar-based jelly, or into a solution, which contains all the nutrients required for its initial germination. As the seedlings develop, they are replated on to new media with different formulations of nutrients, until they are of a size that allows them to be weaned, and established in normal glasshouse conditions.

In vitro cultivation of most hardy orchids using techniques developed for epiphytes has not been very successful. As this group is of minor economic importance, by comparison with the epiphytes, there has been relatively little effort expended upon them until recently. However, research has shown that hardy orchids, particularly the tuber-bearing species, succeed best if grown *in vitro* with their fungal symbionts. This technique improves the growth and development of seedlings, and their subsequent establishment both in standard composts, in gardens, or in the wild. The method is well established with Australian terrestrials, and even saphrophytes such as the Underground Orchid, *Rhizanthella gardneri*, have been flowered from seed. Many thousands of seedlings of both Australian and European terrestrials have already been produced, and the commercial application of these techniques to the latter is eagerly awaited by many growers. Terrestrial orchids are already raised commercially in Australia using symbiotic techniques.

Standard *in vitro* cultivation methods are quite

straightforward, but demand sterile conditions, and equipment beyond what most amateur growers are prepared to devote to their hobby. For an introduction to *in vitro* growing of orchid seedlings refer to Thompson (1977).

In vitro cultivation using symbiotic fungi is rather more complicated by the necessity initially to isolate and culture the appropriate fungus. Research in Australia (Clements 1982) suggests that there is a wide range of specificity in the mycorrhiza/orchid relationship, with some fungi capable of forming mycorrhizal relationships with a range of genera or species. The fungus is obtained from the coils of hyphae which occur in the tissue of orchid roots, where they are digested by the plant. Cultured mycorrhizal fungus is then established on an agar medium and orchid seed is sown on this culture. As it germinates, infection of the protocorm by the symbiont takes place as it would in nature. The fungus then fulfils its role of assisting in nourishing the developing seedling. As the seedling matures it will become green and develop roots, and be capable of independent growth. But the fungus remains with it for the duration of its life *in vitro*, and fulfils an important role at the next stage (see Weaning, below).

This is a very basic account of the mechanisms of *in vitro* symbiotic germination of orchids. For a fuller account refer to Clements (1982).

Weaning seedlings

When weaning terrestrial orchids, it is important to consider the natural development of the plants in question. *Ophrys apifera*, for example, will germinate and develop to two or three leaves, but appears to require cold conditions to initiate tuber production. This requirement might vary from species to species within a genus, and means that the seedlings will have to be removed from their flasks whilst in leaf before a tuber has formed. They will need special weaning conditions as we describe below.

Other genera, such as *Orchis* and *Serapias*, may produce tubers without the requirement for a cold period. These may be transferred to compost as they regrow, which precludes the requirement for weaning, as the new growths will be hardened off

naturally in the greenhouse.

Seedlings grown *in vitro* are typically very soft, having had conditions of ideal temperature and humidity as they develop. They may be weaned to normal growing conditions in the greenhouse, or at cooler times of year indoors. Prior to removal from flasks or tubes, they should be exposed to conditions which will give them the opportunity to begin to harden off. This may be done by removing the lid from the flask or tube, and allowing them a few days to acclimatise to conditions in a propagating case, gradually increasing the amount of air given to them. Otherwise a shady humid spot on a greenhouse bench might be chosen. If seedlings have to be weaned during the winter, they will require supplementary heat to provide a night minimum of at least 10°C (around 48–50°F). During winter, seedlings may best be weaned on a windowsill, in a propagating case.

All seedlings *ex vitro* will be very soft and brittle, and must be handled with the greatest care to avoid bruising tissue, which may provide entry points for fungi and bacteria. At Kew, seedlings grown symbiotically have been found to establish very well when potted initially into community pots, in humid conditions in closed containers with a mixture of sterilised leafmould and perlite. Their development can be monitored by using transparent containers, in order that the growth of roots and tubers may be seen easily. When established they may be hardened off by gradually exposing them to the air. After the first tubers have been formed, and they go into dormancy, they may be potted into their normal mixes and thereafter handled as mature plants.

Epiphytic orchids should be weaned under close, humid and shady conditions, in a compost based on peat, bark and perlite in equal parts, with a particle size of around 7 mm ($^1/_4$ in). Again, initially pot with a number of seedlings in a community pot, gradually increasing the space between the plants until they are large enough to pot individually (when they can be potted into a 62 mm ($2^1/_2$ in) pot). During the winter they will require warm conditions, such as those in a propagating case in a centrally heated room.

Orchids for Particular Places

The lists we give here detail a number of species which are dependable subjects for certain areas in the garden, under the conditions which prevail in southern and western areas of the British Isles. All of these may also be grown in containers, either in frames or in the alpine house. Orchids suitable for growing in lawns and wild gardens are dealt with in the next chapter.

Orchids for bog gardens and marginal areas

This list includes those species which have been grown using the Holman and Whitlow artificial bog techniques.

Cypripedium arietinum
  calceolus var. *parviflorum*
  candidum
  cordigerum
  guttatum
  guttatum var. *yatabeanum*
  macranthum
  reginae

Dactylorhiza majalis
  praetermissa
  purpurella

Epipactis gigantea
  palustris

Orchis laxiflora

Platanthera blepharaglottis
  ciliaris
  psycodes

Spiranthes cernua
  ochroleuca
  romanzoffiana

Orchids for the woodland garden and shady border

By far the most suitable areas for orchids in the garden are those provided by woodland gardens. Some of the finest species one can grow will thrive under these conditions.

Aplectrum hyemale

Calanthe alpina
  discolor
  nipponica
  reflexa
  tricarinata

Cephalanthera falcata

Cymbidium goeringii

Cypripedium acaule
  calceolus (with added lime)
  calceolus var. *pubescens*
  calceolus var. *planipetalum*
  californicum
  candidum
  cordigerum (with added lime)
  debile
  japonicum
  macranthum
  montanum
  reginae

Dactylorhiza elata
   foliosa
   × *grandis*
   praetermissa

Epipactis gigantea

Goodyera (all species)

Liparis krameri
   kumokiri

Orchis mascula

Platanthera dilitata

Pogonia japonica

Spiranthes cernua
   lacera
   ochroleuca
   romanzoffiana

Orchids for the sunny dry border or scree garden

This small group of tuberous terrestrials will survive out of doors in the dry border, but must not be in competition with other more rank-growing plants. Scree conditions suit them very well.

Aceras anthropophorum

Anacamptis pyramidalis

Gymnadenia conopsea

Ophrys apifera
   holoserica

Orchis mascula
   morio

Serapias cordigera

Orchids for the rock garden

It is difficult to select a definitive list of orchids for the rock garden, as so much depends upon the microclimates available to the grower. A well-planned rock garden will incorporate areas with both shady and sunny conditions, moist gullies and perhaps ponds and marginal areas also. In the rock garden one can also create special pockets of soil which will provide perfect conditions for the more specialised species. This list includes a number of species which we have seen to do particularly well in rock gardens. However, most of the species above might be incorporated into a rock garden with the correct aspect and soil type.

Bletilla striata

Cephalanthera longifolia

Coeloglossum viride

Cypripedium calceolus
   reginae

Dactylorhiza × *grandis*
   praetermissa

Epipactis gigantea

Listera ovata

Platanthera bifolia

Spiranthes spiralis

Encouraging Wild Orchids
in the Garden

The minute seeds of orchids provide them with one of the most efficient dispersal mechanisms in the flowering plant kingdom. European terrestrial orchids are often pioneer colonisers of disturbed ground and bare soils, and may appear many kilometres from their nearest known locality. Amongst the most frequent orchids to appear suddenly in unexpected places are the marsh orchids. A large colony of *Dactylorhiza praetermissa, D.fuchsii* and *D.incarnata* sprang up on an abandoned waste dump of clinker at an Essex power station and, within a few years, sported some impressively vigorous natural hybrids of these species. The common Bee Orchid, *Ophrys apifera*, is another that can appear in disturbed habitats well away from its normal preferred sites on the chalk and limestone hills.

The Bee Orchid and the Autumn Ladies' Tresses, *Spiranthes spiralis*, are two of the orchids that most frequently appear apparently spontaneously in lawns, especially in calcareous areas of the country. Careful management of such sites can promote the establishment of sizeable colonies of orchids on lawns. Over a 15-year period, since a solitary rosette was spied in one Oxfordshire garden, a colony of about 130 flowering plants of the Bee Orchid has developed. The owner marks the rosettes in the early spring so that he avoids cutting them with his lawnmower. The patch where they grow is eventually mown in early August well after the plants have set seed and died down. A similar regime has enabled a fine colony of the Green-winged Orchid, *Orchis morio*, to proliferate on the lawns of a convent on Ditchling Common in mid-Sussex. The secret lies in an observant gardener who identifies where the plants are early in the growing season, and allows them to flower and seed unmolested before he mows the site.

The orchids which grow best in lawns are those suited to the environment by their growth habit. Typically, they have rosettes of leaves which begin to grow in the autumn and continue to develop through the winter as the weather permits when competition from other plants is at its least. They have usually formed a new tuber and are ready to flower before the grasses and other herbs have begun to grow strongly.

In the British Isles, the best orchid lawns undoubtedly require a calcareous soil on chalk or limestone. They should never be treated with artificial fertilisers which would cause the orchids to be swamped by the other vegetation and will also interfere with the mycorrhizal association. Any kind of herbicide or moss killer will also certainly kill them rapidly. Even normal lawn operations such as thatching (the removal of dead grass during the autumn) should be avoided and nature left to take its course, apart from mowing at a suitable time of year.

Establishing wild orchids in lawns is a task rendered difficult because they can seldom be obtained in any quantity. If gardening in an area where the orchids grow naturally, changing the management of the lawn may encourage colonisation. The current trend towards wild-flower gardens could provide a suitable habitat where orchids can be encouraged. If a friend has wild orchids in his garden you might be able to obtain fresh seed which might be sprinkled in suitable places. For the best chance of survival, fresh seed should be sown in bare areas devoid of potential competition. However, please remember that you should never take orchids or orchid seed from the wild. Occasionally plants can be obtained when an area has been destroyed for development or a change of land use. These rescue operations are usually carried out by local County Naturalists' Trusts in the UK or Wild Flower Societies in the US, and these bodies should be approached if you feel that you can give a home to some of the rescued material.

Many gardens are bounded by hedgerows and ditches that may be of considerable antiquity. These places often harbour relict populations of orchids and other local plants and are often worth careful study before a management plan is formulated. Again the secret is careful observation to identify what orchids might be present. In overgrown hedges and ditches the orchids may not flower because of the competition from other plants and because of the deep shade that an untended hedge might cast. You must then look out for the leaves usually borne in a rosette that betrays the presence of an orchid. The spotted leaves of the Early Purple Orchid, *Orchis mascula*, and the Common and Heath Spotted Orchids, *Dactylorhiza fuchsii* and *D.maculata*, are readily recognised as are those of the Twayblade, *Listera ovata*. However, the pleated leaves of the Broad-leaved Helleborine, *Epipactis helleborine*, and its rarer allies, and the narrow leaves of the Greater Butterfly Orchid, *Platanthera chlorantha*, are less obvious and need a keen eye to spot them.

All of these species are declining in many parts of the British Isles and are well worth encouraging. Hedgerows are man-made and man-managed habitats. The art of hedge-making is sadly a dying one in Britain but it is currently undergoing something of a revival. A well maintained hedge will not only encourage the orchids growing under it but will also increase the other plant and associated animal and bird life.

Few gardens are large enough nowadays to have a copse or wood within them but again management is the key to maintaining and increasing the diversity of plant and animal life within a wood. Many of the woods of England were an important element in the economy of the area in which they were located. The utilisation of many of these involved a system of coppicing the wood on a rotational basis. Coppicing involved cutting hazel, hornbeam or chestnut back to the base thereby opening up the wood. These trees sprout again from the base and in a few years establish a continuous canopy again with consequent reduction of the light levels. In the seasons immediately following coppicing, orchids and other herbaceous elements of the woodland ground flora burst into flower producing an abundance of seed for future generations. Sadly many woods in this country have been neglected for many years and consequently their ground flora and orchids have declined or even disappeared.

Classification

In such a large family as the orchids it is useful to understand a little of how they have been classified, because a knowledge of the relationships of orchid genera can have useful predictive value for the orchid grower.

The 20,000 or so species of orchids fall into about 900 genera which in turn have been grouped into subtribes, tribes and subfamilies in ascending order. The most recent fully published classification of the orchids is that of Dressler (1981) and it will be followed here. Dressler and his predecessors have attempted to group similar orchids together and to show how these groups are related to each other. The theory of evolution has provided a rationale for attempting to construct classifications of related groups and most recent classifications have attempted to suggest evolutionary relationships.

Most classifications of orchids have concentrated upon features of the flowers, especially of the sexual parts, to provide clues as to relationships. Dressler has also supplied much additional information from vegatative morphology, anatomy, cytology and micromorphology to substantiate his classification. He divides the orchids into six subfamilies; Apostasioideae, Cypripedioideae, Spiranthoideae, Orchidoideae, Epidendroideae and Vandoideae. Genera in all of these, except the primitive tropical Asiatic Apostasioideae, are included in this book. We list below these genera in their appropriate subfamilies and tribes and encourage readers to study their orchids closely to give them some insight into the relationships suggested here.

Subfamily **Cypripedioideae**

Cypripedium

Subfamily **Spiranthoideae**
    Tribe Erythrodeae
        Subtribe Goodyerinae   *Goodyera*
    Tribe Cranichidae
        Subtribe Spiranthinae   *Spiranthes*

Subfamily **Orchidoideae**
    Tribe Neottieae
        Subtribe Limodorinae   *Cephalanthera, Epipactis*
        Subtribe Listerinae   *Listera*
    Tribe Diurideae
        Subtribe Chloraeinae   *Chloraea*
        Subtribe Caladeniineae   *Caladenia*
        Subtribe Pterostyliidnae   *Pterostylis*
        Subtribe Acianthinae   *Acianthus, Corybas*
        Subtribe Diuridinae   *Diuris, Thelymitra*
    Tribe Orchidieae
        Subtribe Orchidinae   *Ceologlossum, Dactylorhiza, Platanthera, Gymnadenia, Aceras, Amitostigma, Barlia, Himantoglos: Comperia, Orchis, Anacamptis, Ophrys, Serapias*
        Subtribe Habenariinae   *Habenaria*
    Tribe Diseae
        Subtribe Diseae   *Disa*
        Subtribe Satyriinae   *Satyrium*

Subfamily **Epidendroideae**
  Tribe Vanilleae
    Subtribe Pogoniinae   *Pogonia*
  Tribe Arethusae
    Subtribe Arethusinae   *Arethusa*
    Subtribe Bletiinae   *Bletilla,*
                      Calanthe,
                      Calopogon
  Tribe Coelogyninae
    Subtribe Coelogyninae   *Pleione*
  Tribe Malaxideae   *Liparis,*
                      Malaxis

  Tribe Calypsoeae   *Calypso,*
                      Dactylostalix
  Tribe Epidendreae
    Subtribe Dendrobiinae *Dendrobium*

Subfamily **Vandoideae**
  Tribe Maxillariea
    Subtribe Corallorhizinae *Cremastra,*
                      Oreorchis,
                      Aplectrum
    Subtribe Cyrtopodiinae *Cymbidium*

Catalogue of Orchids

ACERAS

A monotypic genus closely allied to *Orchis* but distinguished by the lip which lacks a spur.

A.anthropophorum (L.)R.Br.
(FIGURE 11A)

The Man Orchid gets its name from the flower, which has a lip whose outline is suggestive of that of a hanging man. It is by no means a showy orchid growing to about 25 or 30 cm tall, with a slender dense spike of many small green flowers, with a yellow or reddish-brown lip about 7–10 mm long.

It is a local plant in southern and central England but widespread on the Continent. In Britain it grows in chalk or limestone grassland, and elsewhere is always associated with calcareous soils usually in open places in grassland and scrub or on the edges of woodland.

It is an easy subject for the garden and in pot-culture. Compost C (see p.27) with added dolomite chips suits it well.

In the wild it hybridises with several species of *Orchis* and the offspring are often very attractive plants. For example, hybrids with *O.simia* and *O.militaris* are not uncommon on the continent and both are showy and vigorous plants worth cultivating.

ACIANTHUS

A small Australasian genus of about 20 species, *Acianthus* is similar in its habit to *Corybas* having a single heart-shaped leaf subtending the inflorescence. However, it has an inflorescence of several small flowers in a lax spike. Only a few species are at all easy to cultivate. They are best grown in pots in the alpine house, using compost E (see p.27) or an open mix of silica sand and leafmould.

A.caudatus R.Br.
(FIGURE 12A)

This is the most striking species in the genus reaching 20 cm tall in well-grown specimens. It has a heart-shaped dark green leaf with a deep purple lower surface. The spidery dark maroon flowers have a long slender tapering sepals 2–3.5 cm long and much shorter petals and lip. The flowers have a strange and unpleasant scent of dogs.

It grows in shaded situations under trees and shrubs in coastal areas of eastern Australia from New South Wales to South Australia. It flowers from August to October in the wild.

A.exsertus R.Br.

The Mosquito Orchid is a dainty plant a few cm tall with a 3 cm long heart-shaped leaf, dark purple on the lower surface. Three to twenty flowers are borne in an open spike. Each flower is about 8 cm long and greenish-white flushed with purple.

It is a widespread and abundant species in coastal areas of eastern Australia, often forming large colonies. It has proved an easy orchid to grow and multiply in pot-culture.

Figure 11
A, *Aceras anthropophorum*;   **B**, *Barlia robertiana*

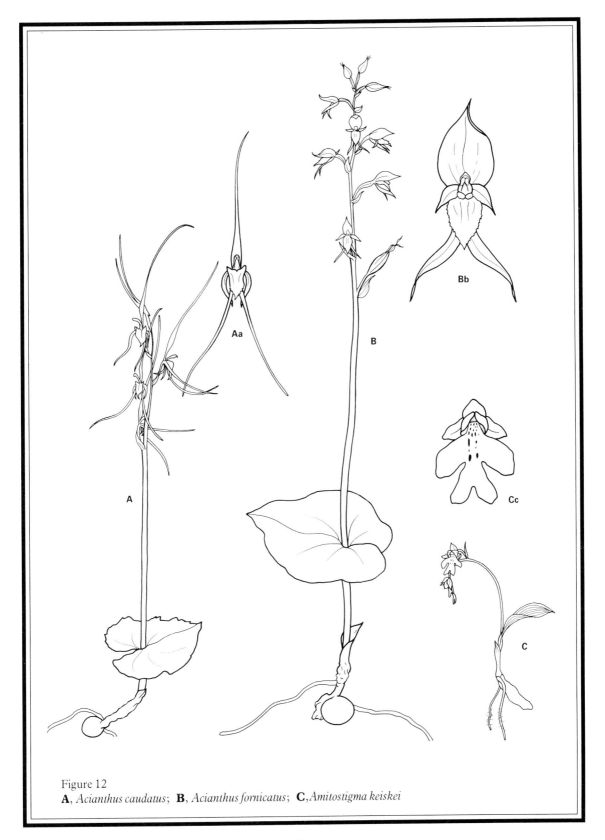

Figure 12
A, *Acianthus caudatus*; **B**, *Acianthus fornicatus*; **C**,*Amitostigma keiskei*

A.fornicatus R.Br.

(FIGURE 12B)

This dainty orchid has the delightful common name in Australia of Pixie Caps. It is a tiny plant with an ovate or cordate leaf, dark green above and purple beneath, about 3 cm long. It can have up to 14 flowers about 1 cm long in a lax spike. The flowers are whitish-green with a purple flush on the sepals.

It is a widespread orchid that forms sizeable colonies throughout eastern Australia. It does well in cultivation and multiplies freely in the pots.

AMITOSTIGMA

A small genus of dwarf orchids closely allied to *Ponerorchis* and *Dactylorhiza* with about 30 species in the eastern Himalaya, China and Japan. Few are ever seen in cultivation outside Japan.

A.keiskei (Max.)Schltr.

(FIGURE 12C)

The largest-flowered of the Japanese species, *A.keiskei* is a gem that will produce sizeable colonies in the right conditions. It is a tiny plant 5 to 12 cm tall with 1 to 3 flowers, 1 cm across, borne at the apex of a slender stem. The flowers have a deeply four-lobed lip with a short spur a few mm long at the base. Two rows of deep purple spots lead to the mouth of the spur. The inflorescence is subtended by a single suberect ligulate leaf on the slender stem. A white-flowered form is occasionally seen in the wild and in cultivation.

Given its tiny size, this species is best placed at eye-level for its beauty to be appreciated. In the wild it grows in wet mossy places on rocks and in boggy places in the mountains of central Japan and should, therefore, be grown in a damp peaty compost. It is best suited to pot-culture in an alpine house, using compost D (see p.27). A shady humid spot in the house will suit it best.

ANACAMPTIS

A monotypic genus whose single species is the well-known Pyramidal Orchid, *A.pyramidalis*. It is a common species in chalk and limestone grassland, distributed throughout Europe and extending into Asia.

A.pyramidalis (L.)L.C.Rich

(FIGURE 13A)

The compact pyramidal head of rich purple flowers makes this orchid one of the easiest identifiable of the European species. On the Continent, pale pink-flowered forms often predominate and white-flowered plants are not uncommon. The individual flowers are small, a few mm across, with a three-lobed lip and a slender spur 12–14 mm long at its base. They are similar to those of the Fragrant Orchid, *Gymnadenia conopsea*. However, they have short basal calli on each side of the mouth of the spur not found in the latter.

The Pyramidal Orchid occasionally turns up in lawns in calcareous areas and makes a good subject for a sunny border. It can also be grown in pots in compost C (see p.27) to which limestone or dolomite chips should be added.

APLECTRUM

A small genus of two species, the well-known *A.hyemale* from North America and *A.unguiculatum* from Japan. The genus is allied to *Cremastra*. It is characterised by its bulbous tubers connected by a slender rhizome, one or two leaves and a flower with free sepals and petals, a three-lobed lip with a callus of lamellate crests and an anther with two pairs of pollinia.

A.hyemale (Willd.)Nuttall

(FIGURE 14A)

The common names of this orchid are Putty Foot and Adam and Eve, the former acquired for the ability of its tubers to produce a glue used to stick broken pots. The plant produces a single elliptic pleated leaf, beautifully veined with silver, which has died down by the time the flowering spike appears. This reaches 50 cm tall and bears 6 to 10 small flowers. The sepals and petals are yellow to greenish with violet or brown tips, and the lip is white with purple markings.

Figure 13
A, *Anacamptis pyramidalis*; **B**, *Coeloglossum viride*; **C**, *Gymnadenia conopsea*

Figure 14
A, *Aplectrum hyemale*; **B**, *Arethusa bulbosa*; **C**, *Bletilla striata*

It is found in the north-eastern part of the United States and in adjacent Canada, where it grows in deep shade in leaf litter on the forest floor. Case (1987) says that it is an amenable subject in cultivation. It should be grown under woodland garden conditions, or in compost D (see p. 27) in containers in a shady frame or in the alpine house.

ARETHUSA

A monotypic genus with its single species, *A. bulbosa*. in North America.

A.bulbosa L.
(FIGURE 14B)

This dwarf species produces a single flower or rarely two at the apex of a slender stalk, up to 40 cm long, before the solitary lanceolate leaf appears. The flower adopts a perky stance with erect rose-pink sepals and petals and a three-lobed lip which is geniculately bent in the middle. The lip is purple-spotted and bears a central bright yellow bearded crest. A rare albino form can sometimes be found in the wild.

A. bulbosa flowers in the spring or early summer in its native habitat of wet peat and *Sphagnum* bogs, where it can grow almost aquatically in floating moss rafts. It often forms small colonies in the wild. In cultivation it is a tricky subject and is usually short-lived, flowering once before it disappears altogether. It should be grown in a pot in peat and living *Sphagnum* that is kept moist at all times (see growing bog orchids in containers, p. 23).

BARLIA

A small genus of one or possibly two species, *Barlia* is closely related to *Himantoglossum* but differs in having a much shorter and differently shaped lip, neither probably sufficient reason for this split!

B.robertiana (Loisel.)Greuter
(FIGURE 11B)

The Giant Orchid is one of the earliest flowering of the Mediterranean orchids, bursting into flower in January in Cyprus and Crete but a month or so later farther north. Well-grown plants reach 70 or 80 cm tall but 30 to 50 cm is more common. The plants have several broad, shiny, palish green leaves and a dense cylindrical inflorescence of many fragrant flowers. These are 3.5 to 4.5 cm long and are dominated by their four-lobed somewhat humanoid lip. The lip is white variously marked with pink or purple and with a narrow to broad greenish or brownish margin.

This is another of the calcicolous orchids found on grassy hillsides, amongst scrub and in clearings in woodland. The form that is found in the Canary Islands has been treated as a distinct species by some authors, but we consider it to fall within the range of variation found elsewhere in *B. robertiana*. An imposing subject for pot cultivation in compost C (see p. 27) with added lime.

BLETILLA

This small genus of about three species from Eastern Asia should not be confused with the similar tropical American genus *Bletia*, which is unsuitable as a subject for the garden or an alpine house. The best known species, *B. striata*, is one of the finest hardy orchids, and also one of the easiest to obtain in the nursery trade.

B.striata (Thunb.)Reichb.f.
(FIGURE 14C)

The well-known Hyacinth Orchid gains its name from its 3 to 6 sweetly-scented rose-purple flowers which are carried towards the apex of a slender erect or arching scape, 30–45 cm tall. The inflorescence rises above the pleated lanceolate leaves which are produced from a depressed underground tuberous pseudobulb. Pale pink and white-flowered forms are not uncommon and, to our taste, are prettier than the more typical form with its orchid-purple flowers. It is still sometimes sold under the later name *B. hyacinthina*.

This delightful orchid is native to China and Japan where it is found at elevations up to 3,200 m (10,500 ft), growing on the margins of woods and thickets. It prefers a sheltered spot in light shade or in full sun where the loamy humus-rich soil is well-drained. It will form large colonies if left undisturbed for a few years. The drift of Hyacinth Orchid alongside the old Ferneries at Kew in full flower in June was one of the early summer treats in the Gardens. On the Continent, it is occasionally seen in landscaped gardens where its pleated leaves are as much a feature as its flowers throughout the summer months. It is also sometimes grown there on larger rock gardens. It makes a good subject in pots in colder areas where it can be brought indoors during the winter. Compost A or D (see p. 26–7) will suit it well.

CALADENIA

It is a shame that most of the species of this large genus of predominantly Australian orchids have proved difficult to grow. Some of the species are amongst the showiest of the Australian native species. The best composts to use are those based on acidic sandy loams with a high proportion of leafmould, plus grit for sharp drainage. Plastic pots have generally given better results than clay ones. A full account of the cultivated species is given by Elliot & Jones (1982). In Britain they will require temperatures at the warmer end of the alpine house's range, 4–5°C (39–41°F) minimum.

C.deformis R.Br.
(FIGURE 15C)

This is a small terrestrial species, 5 to 15 cm tall with a slender slightly hairy basal leaf 8 to 12 cm long. The flower is 2 to 3 cm across and usually a striking blue, although pink and white forms are known. The fringed lip is much smaller than the sepals and petals and has a darker callus of several dissected ridges.

C.deformis is widespread in coastal areas in both eastern and south-western Australia where it grows in small clumps in sandy places.

C.dilatata R.Br.
(FIGURE 15A)

This handsome Spider Orchid is well worth trying. It is an elegant plant 15 to 45 cm tall with a lanceolate, hairy basal leaf up to 12 cm long. The solitary flower looks upwards and can measure up to 10 cm across. It is green and tinted with yellow and purple.

It is widespread in eastern and south-western Australia, growing in sandy soils in open forest and heathland. There are several similar species in Western Australia but these have proved difficult in cultivation.

C.flava R.Br.
(FIGURE 15D)

This pretty Western Australian species is called the Cowslip Orchid. It is a colonial species growing to about 25 cm tall, with a hairy basal leaf up to 25 cm long. The flowers, 3.5 to 4.5 cm across, are yellow and sometimes flecked with red.

In the wild it grows in deep sandy soils and should be cultivated in a very sandy mix; compost E (see p. 27) with extra sharp sand should suit it well.

C.menziesii R.Br.
(FIGURE 15B)

This is the Common Spider Orchid of Australia. It is a small-flowered species but the most willing in cultivation. It grows to about 20 cm tall with an ovate-lanceolate glabrous leaf at the base. The stalk carries 1 to 3 purple and white flowers, 1.5 to 2.5 cm across, and resembling a small rabbit head with the petals the ears.

It is common in coastal areas in sandy soils and can form congested colonies. It prefers a sandy mix in cultivation and should be overpotted.

CALANTHE

Calanthe is one of the larger genera of terrestrial orchids with about 200 species widespread in south-eastern and eastern Asia, Africa, Madagascar and the Pacific Islands, with one species in the

Figure 15
A, *Caladenia dilatata*; **B**, *C. menziesii*; **C**, *C. deformis*; **D**, *C. flava*

tropical Americas and another in Australia. Most calanthes grow on the floors of tropical or subtropical forests, but in the Far East a few are found in temperate woodland and these species are hardy or half-hardy. Among these and their hybrids are some of the most rewarding of all gardenworthy orchids. All of the Japanese and Chinese species are evergreen. A few of the Himalayan species are also worth growing but are less commonly seen in Britain.

In Japan, the cultivation of calanthes is a pastime that warrants its own society, the Japanese Calanthean Society (address, p. 123). Undoubtedly, the popularity of these orchids is partly due to the wide variety of form and colour now available as a result of the large number of hybrids that are in cultivation. Most of these are man-made but natural hybrids do occur and some of these have also been introduced into cultivation. All calanthes will grow in compost D (see p.27), and equally well in compost A (see p.26) with added peat to make it more moisture-retentive. Some are good garden plants, and all will do well in containers.

C.alpina Hook.f.
(FIGURE 16B)

The flowers of *C.alpina* do not open widely. Between 3 and 8 are borne on a 20–25 cm long stalk which emerges from between the pleated leaves. The flowers are lilac-coloured with an orangish lip which has a frilled mid-lobe and an ascending tapering spur at its base.

Like *C.tricarinata*, this attractive species has to survive a covering of snow in the winter in its natural habitat. It is a widespread species from Sikkim, where it is found up to 3,000 m (9,840 ft), in China, Taiwan and Japan. At these altitudes, it must tolerate hot summers and cold winters. In Japan, where it is known under its synonym of *C.schlechteri*, it grows in shade in forest at 1,300–1,500 m (4,265–4,920 ft).

C.aristulifera Reichb.f.

This is one of the most graceful calanthes with several nodding lilac-coloured flowers borne on 30–40 cm tall spikes, which emerge between the young leaves of the new growth. Its flowers do not open widely and have a long slender upwards pointing spur emerging from the base of the lip.

Calanthe aristulifera occurs on the southern islands as far north as southern Honshu. It grows on rocks and decaying tree trunks along streams in laurel forests and also in *Cryptomeria japonica* plantations. It requires more humidity than *C.striata*. In the garden it can be grown in a peaty loam mix with added leafmould, in a shaded and sheltered position, but is only hardy in the mildest parts of Britain and elsewhere should be grown in a greenhouse. It hybridises with *C.discolor* and *C.striata* in the wild. Both its natural and artificial hybrids with hardier species are easier to grow.

C.discolor Lindley
(FIGURE 17B)

This attractive orchid is probably the most widely available in trade. It is a striking plant when in flower, with 20–50 cm tall inflorescences emerging from between the developing leaves. These bear a cylindrical head of up to 20 flowers, each 2 cm across, with chocolate-brown sepals and petals and a pink lip. It was one of Thunberg's earliest collections in Japan where it is widely distributed throughout the islands. It is also found in Korea and mainland China. In nature it grows in colonies in fairly damp grassy places, and in forest on the lower parts of the mountains.

In cultivation it is one of the most tolerant species, and will survive out of doors in a sheltered sunny or partly shaded spot in peaty loam. It much appreciates a generous mulch of leafmould.

C.izu-insularis Ohwi & Satomi

This is similar to *C.discolor* and may be only a geographical variant, but it has a larger flower with rose-pink sepals and petals and a white lip with a bright yellow spot at the base. It is found only on the Izu Islands off the south coast of the main island of Honshu.

C.izu-insularis needs the protection of the alpine house in the British Isles and likes a humid, well-aerated environment. It should never be allowed to dry out. *C.Kozu*, its natural hybrid

Figure 16
A, *Calanthe reflexa*; **B**, *C.alpina* **C**, *C.nipponica*

with *C.discolor*, is a popular plant in cultivation being easier to grow and more vigorous than its parents.

C.longicalcarata Hayata

An attractive orchid which flowers as the new leaves are produced in the spring. It has 15 to 20 delicate lilac or less commonly white flowers in a lax inflorescence. The lip is three-lobed with a short broad mid-lobe, spreading falcate side lobes and an ascending slender spur about 1.5 cm long. The callus comprises several low irregular ridges.

This species is found in the southern islands of Japan and the Ryukyu Islands. It reaches its most northerly point in the Izu Islands to the east of the main Japanese island of Honshu. It is a late-flowering species from July until mid-August.

C.longicalcarata hybridises in nature with *C.furcata* and *C.japonica*.

C.nipponica Makino
(FIGURE 16C)

This attractive orchid is a true alpine in Japan but it has a reputation for being difficult to grow.

C.nipponica is one of the smaller species reaching 30 cm tall. The plant produces a laxly few-flowered inflorescence above its 3–5 pleated dark green leaves. The flowers are nutant and have pale green spreading sepals and petals and a lemon-yellow lip sometimes marked with orange at the base. The basal oblong callus has an erose margin.

In the wild it grows in shaded spots in deep leaf litter in woodland.

C.reflexa Max.
(FIGURE 16A)

A graceful species with delicate lavender and off-white flowers borne on a 30–50 cm long stalk above the spreading lanceolate pleated leaves. It has acuminate reflexed sepals and petals, and a narrow three-lobed lip with a large apiculate obovate mid-lobe and a short reflexed spur at the base. A white-flowered form is a rarity in the wild.

This is a widespread species from the Himalayas to Taiwan and Japan, up to about 2,500 m (8,200 ft) elevation. It usually grows in swampy ground or in moist cool woodland and prefers a peaty loam mixed with leafmould in a sheltered shady position in the garden. It flowers late in the season into the early autumn. Warm weather can lead to bud fall if the plants are not shaded or if air pollution is bad.

C.striata (Sw.)R.Br.
(FIGURE 17A)

This is perhaps better known under the later synonym *C.sieboldii*. It is closely allied to *C.discolor* but differs in having larger yellow flowers with either yellow or reddish-brown sepals and petals. The lip, like that of *C.discolor*, is broadly three-lobed with each lobe somewhat spathulate and spreading.

It is less hardy than *C.discolor* and probably requires protection in a greenhouse over the winter. It is native in Taiwan and in southern Japan at altitudes up to 800 m where it grows in laurel forests, and flowers in April and May.

C.Takane, a natural hybrid of *C.striata* with *C.discolor*, is popular in cultivation. It has slightly scented flowers the size of *C.striata* but the colour of *C.discolor*.

C.tricarinata Lindley
(FIGURE 17C)

A widespread species found all the way from the Himalayas to Taiwan and Japan. Plants in cultivation in the British Isles mainly come from Japan. *C.tricarinata* flowers as the young leaves emerge, sending up a stout spike up to 45 cm tall, carrying many subcampanulate flowers with green sepals and petals and a crimson to brick-red lip, which has a pale yellow base. The lip is three-lobed with a broadly subcircular mid-lobe with an undulate margin and a callus of three raised longitudinal ridges running from the base to the apex.

The leaves tend to fray and tear as the season progresses, as in many calanthes, to produce an

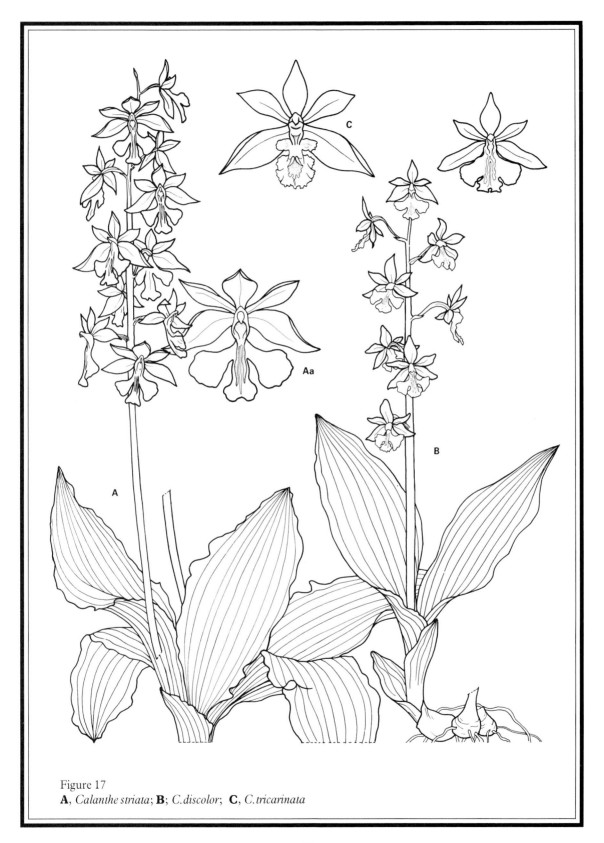

Figure 17
A, *Calanthe striata*; **B**; *C.discolor*; **C**, *C.tricarinata*

untidy plant unless some cosmetic surgery is undertaken. At Kew, we have grown *C.tricarinata* for some years on a raised peat bed near the Alpine House, where it is lightly shaded and protected from the worst of the winter weather.

In the wild it can be found up to 3,000 m (9,840 ft) or more in the Himalayas and south-western China. One of us has seen it growing in the mountains of north-western Yunnan in shaded damp places in wooded gulleys in deep leaf litter. In Japan it is found from about 400–1,000 m (1,310–3,280 ft) in beech woodland.

Natural hybrids of *C.tricarinata* with *C.discolor*, *C.striata* and *C.aristulifera* have all been recorded, the first being rather frequent. All are in cultivation and are occasionally available in the British Isles.

CALOPOGON

The genus *Calopogon* comprises four species, all from North America. It is related to *Arethusa* but is distinguished by its nonresupinate flowers, distinctive erect bearded lip and elongate column, winged at the apex. Only one species, *C.tuberosus*, is a suitable subject for cultivation.

C.tuberosus (L.)Britton, Sterns & Pogg.
(FIGURE 18D)

This attractive species is very variable in size ranging from 7.5 to 120 cm in height. It grows from an ovoid tuber, about 2 cm across, which produces 1 to 5 basal, linear-lanceolate, ribbed leaves from which emerge an erect slender scape bearing 3 to 25 flowers. The upturned, 3.5 to 4.4 cm- wide flowers are very showy with spreading pink sepals and petals, and a pink lip with a yellow spot at the apex of the bearded apex of the callus. Albino forms are not uncommon in the wild.

C.tuberosus is widespread in North America from Newfoundland south to Florida and also in the northern Caribbean. It grows in bogs, with the tuber either in live *Sphagnum* or else deep in sandy soil. In cultivation, it is one of the species that can be grown in live *Sphagnum* moss in a container.

CALYPSO

A monotypic genus widespread in north temperate regions from North America across northern Europe and Asia to Japan.

C.bulbosa (L.)Oakes
(FIGURE 18C)

The dainty and delightful Calypso Orchid has a small underground tuber that produces a basal pleated ovate 3 to 6 cm long leaf, with an undulate margin, on a long petiole and an erect one-flowered inflorescence on a slender reddish stalk. The slender tapering pink sepals and petals are erect and spreading. Its lip is distinctive, saccate at the base with a flat ovate apical lobe and two appressed spurs as long as the lip. The white or very pale pink lip is marked with purple streaks in the basal half and has a white or yellow tuft of hairs at the base of the apical lobe.

Three varieties have been recognised. The typical variety is found in northern Scandinavia and throughout Asia to Japan. The other two are North American and both have leaves with smooth margins and spurs that exceed the lip in length. Var.*americana* is the prettiest with a large yellow callus tuft and a weakly spotted apical lobe to the lip. Var.*occidentalis* has a duller flower with a white callus tuft and an apical lobe mottled and irregularly blotched with purple.

In the wild, Calypso grows in damp places and marshes in coniferous forests, usually in wet moss and rotting leaf litter at the base of trees.

Calypso starts into growth in the autumn and therefore needs alpine house conditions. It should be grown in a very open 'fluffy' mix of leafmould and crushed quartzite grit or in living *Sphagnum* moss in a container. The plants should be kept moist in growth but should be allowed to dry out somewhat in the summer in a shaded frame.

CEPHALANTHERA

Cephalanthera is a relatively large genus of terrestrial orchids in Europe, Asia and Japan. With *Epipactis* they are called Helleborines in the British Isles. Two native species, the Common Helleb-

Figure 18
A, *Eleorchis japonica* **B**, *Dactylostalix ringens*; **C**, *Calypso bulbosa*; **D**, *Calopogon tuberosus*

orine, *C.damasonium* (Figure 19C, p.69) and the Sword-leaved Helleborine, *C.longifolia*, are white-flowered. The Red Helleborine, *C.rubra* (Figure 19B, p.69) as its name suggests has rose-red flowers. It is also one of the rarest orchids, known only from a few places, in all of which only a few plants remain. Fortunately, it is a common orchid on the Continent. None of the native species is in general cultivation in Britain, although the white-flowered species occasionally turn up in gardens under old hedges, especially in chalky areas. They should grow well in containers in compost C (see p.27) with added limestone. Those trying to grow these helleborines should note that the rhizomes are thin and dry out rapidly when removed from the soil.

C.falcata (Thunb.)Blume

An erect terrestrial 25–30 cm tall with five or six suberect lancelate-elliptic and acuminate leaves. The flowers are erect, about 1.5 cm long, and do not open widely. The lip has a very short conical spur at the base.

This species is not unlike *C.damasonium* but it has bright lemon-yellow rather than white flowers. It is another Japanese species that grows in nature in shaded places. At Kew it has been grown in an open peaty loam with added leafmould in a sheltered shaded position.

C.kurdica Bornm.
(FIGURE 19A)

This delightful orchid is the only species in the genus that can produce sizeable clumps of up to 20 stems in the wild. It can grow to 50 cm tall, with relatively short dull green leaves and a dense spike of pretty pink flowers with a creamy lip. Rich purple-flowered forms are rare, but spectacular while albinos are commoner but undistinguished.

C.kurdica as its name suggests is a common species in southern and eastern Turkey across to Iran. It grows in shade in Pine woods, and in scrub on limestone in the mountains from about 800–2,100 m (2,625–3,935 ft) elevation. Compost D (see p.27) with added limestone and alpine house cultivation is recommended.

CHLORAEA

The temperate South American terrestrial genus *Chloraea* undoubtedly deserves greater attention from growers. There are several very showy orchids amongst its 85 or so species. A few of these have been in cultivation in the British Isles and have thrived for a few years before being lost.

Chloraea is distinguished by its fleshy cylindrical roots, and by its flowers in which the lip is usually papillose, has a basal callus of ridges and lacks a spur.

The following are examples of some of the more attractive species in the genus. We recommend they be grown in pots in compost C or D (see p.27) in the alpine house.

C.crispa Lindl.
(FIGURE 20C)

One of the larger species, *C.crispa* grows from 30 to 90 cm tall and has several oblanceolate basal leaves topped by a subdense inflorescence of few to many flowers. These are large and white with green spots on the side lobes of the lip and an orange-brown mark at the base of the column. The sepals are about 3 to 3.5 cm long. The oblong lip is strongly recurved with a crispate margin and callus of 7 to 9 fimbriate lamellae.

It grows on sandy plains in Chile and was first flowered in Britain at Kew in April 1903, and figured in the *Botanical Magazine* (t.7955).

C.longibracteata Lindl.
(FIGURE 20B)

This is a smaller species than the preceding one reaching about 45 cm tall. The rather fleshy elliptic-obovate leaves are borne in a basal rosette from which emerges the many-flowered inflorescence. The flowers are predominantly white but the sepals have deep green horn-like tips, and the lip has yellow side lobes, veined with green. The callus consists of 7 short verrucose ridges.

This species is found in coastal Chile where it grows in shallow soils of crumbling granitic sand, in sparse scrub with scattered grasses and bulbs.

This species is considered to be a species of *Gavilea* by some authorities.

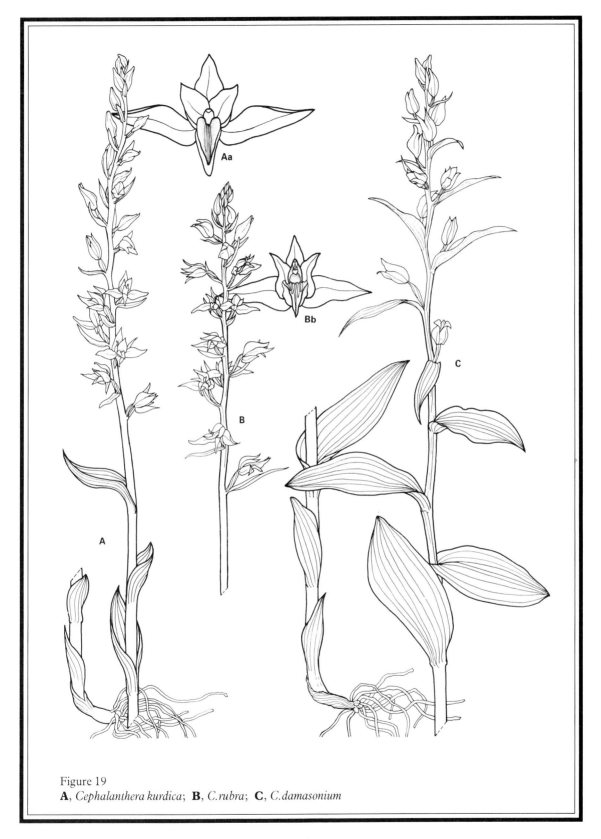

Figure 19
A, *Cephalanthera kurdica*; **B**, *C.rubra*; **C**, *C.damasonium*

69

Figure 20
A, *Chloraea gavilu*; **B**, *C.longibracteata*; **C**, *C.crispa*

C.virescens (Willd.)Lindl.

Another attractive orchid that grows to 45 cm tall from a basal cluster of 6 to 8 oblanceolate ascending leaves. The inflorescence bears several showy white or pale yellow flowers with greenish tips to the sepals and green papillae on the lip. The sepals are 2 to 2.5 cm long and the obscurely three-lobed recurved lip 1.6 to 2 cm long. The callus comprises 5 basal ridges and the veins in front are embellished with short falcate papillae.

This species first flowered in Britain in 1849 at the Birmingham Botanic Garden. It has also been flowered at Kew, in 1903, having been introduced the previous year by H.J. Elwes from Chile. It grows in the wild in sandy plains near the coast.

C.gavilu Lindl. (Figure 20A, p.70) has been confused with this species but differs in its bright yellow flowers and papillate tips to the sepals.

COELOGLOSSUM

A monotypic genus whose only species, the Frog Orchid. *C.viride*, is one of the most widespread and least spectacular of all temperate orchids.

C.viride (L.)Hartm.
(FIGURE 13B)

The Frog Orchid grows from a digitate tuber producing a few elliptic or ovate fleshy leaves along the stem, which can reach 20 cm or more but is often only a few cm tall. The flowers are green with varying degrees of brown or maroon flushing on the oblong lip that is obscurely three-lobed at the apex.

This orchid is widely distributed throughout north temperate areas and is one of the few orchids found within the Arctic Circle and in the frozen wastes of Greenland and Iceland. It is a tolerant plant in nature found in a variety of habitats from woodland to open grassland. It occasionally can be found in lawns in old gardens, especially in chalk areas. In cultivation it should be grown in compost C (see p.27) with added limestone or dolomite chips, and may succeed in the garden given good drainage and extra limestone chips.

COMPERIA

Comperia is a monotypic genus allied to *Himantoglossum* and is certainly one of the most spectacular of the orchids of the Middle East. It differs from *Himantoglossum* in its distinctive lip shape. Sadly it is declining rapidly as it is dug up in large quantities for salep and salep ice-cream.

C.comperiana (Steven)Asch. & Graebn. (FIGURE 21A)

Comper's Orchid is a large orchid, 30 to 70 cm tall, with 3 to 6 glossy yellow-green basal leaves. The stout stalk carries a few large flowers. The sepals and petals form a large 1.5 to 2 cm long hood over the column. The deflexed lip is fan-shaped in the whitish or pale pink basal part from which hang three long slender threads up to 4 cm long.

It is a rare species in Europe known only from a few of the eastern Aegean Islands but is more frequent in Turkey and the Middle East. It grows in deciduous and coniferous woodlands on limestone, often in very dry areas. It is best grown in a pot in the alpine house in compost C (see p.27 with added limestone or dolomite chips.

CORYBAS

About 60 species of *Corybas* are known, distributed from South-East Asia through the Malay Archipelago to the Pacific Islands, Australia and New Zealand. Only a few of the Australian and New Zealand species are suitable subjects for cultivation.

The genus is a particularly distinctive one. The plants are tiny with a solitary orbicular or heart-shaped leaf growing from a small tuber. The single flower is large for the size of the plant and can either sit on the leaf or be borne on a short stalk above it. The flower has a conspicuously hooded dorsal sepal, short to long thread-like lateral sepals and petals, and a strongly recurved lip which can be two-spurred at the base.

They are best grown in a pot in compost E (see p.27) with added well-rotted leafmould, with the tubers placed 2 to 3 cm below the soil surface.

Figure 21

A, *Comperia comperiana*; **B**, *Himantoglossum hircinum*

They should not be allowed to dry out during the growing season and some can benefit from the high humidity created under a bell jar or similar cover. A full account of all of the Australian species in cultivation is given by Elliot & Jones (1984).

C.dilatatus (Rupp & Nicholls) Rupp & Nicholls (FIGURE 22A)

This dwarf species has an orbicular green leaf, 1.5 to 2 cm across, and a short-stalked flower that appears to sit on the leaf surface. The flowers are translucent with a central pure white area in the mouth of the lip and striped with purple on the margins and dorsal sepal. The lateral sepals and petals are inconspicuous but the lip is large with a spreading dentate margin.

It is a common orchid in eastern and south-western Australia, growing in damp sheltered places. In cultivation it should not be allowed to dry out during the growing season.

C.orbiculatus (Col.) L.B. Moore

One of the rarer species from New Zealand, it is not unlike *C.rivularis* in overall flower shape, particularly the slender elongate petals and lateral sepals that spread from behind the lip. However, the lip is rounder with a dark purple throat and the dorsal sepal is obtuse rather than truncate at the apex. It grows in shaded damp places throughout Britain and in Stewart and Chatham Islands, flowering from early to late spring.

C.pruinosus (R. Cunn.)Reichb.f.

A species with a bright green orbicular leaf and greyish-green flower marked with purple. The lip opens widely and is edged with conspicuous red and white lacerate teeth.

It is a species endemic to the central parts of New South Wales. It grows and flowers freely in cultivation preferring a loamier substrate than most other species.

C.fimbriatus (Figure 22B, p. 74) is similar but has a heart-shaped leaf with a larger flower, up to 3 cm long, and more prominent lip. It is an east-ern Australian species common in coastal areas where it will often produce large colonies. It grows well in a sandy soil mix containing plenty of leaf-mould and needs a humid spot to prevent bud drop.

C.trilobus (Hook.F.) Reichb.f. (FIGURE 22C)

This dainty little orchid is the commonest species in New Zealand. It grows to no more than 6 cm tall and has a broadly cordate apiculate leaf, 2 to 2.5 cm across, which is green and blotched with purple. The shortly stalked dull purple flower has a blunt hooded dorsal sepal and erect elongate slenderly ribbon-like lateral sepals and petals, giving the flower a spidery appearance. The short broad lip is strongly recurved and has an erose margin.

It grows under Southern Beech and in bush in relatively dry or wet sites where it can form large colonies. It flowers in early to late spring, between June and November, in its native habitats.

CREMASTRA

Cremastra is a small but choice genus of three species from eastern and south-eastern Asia. Only one of these is common in cultivation.

C.appendiculata (Don)Makino (FIGURE 29B)

This elegant orchid produces a single pleated lanceolate leaf which arises from an onion-like, shallowly buried pseudobulb, itself attached to a string of older pseudobulbs from previous years. In its habit it shows clear affinities with *Eulophia*. The inflorescence rises to 45 cm tall on a stout purplish stalk with a dense cylindrical head of slender, nodding, lilac- and flesh-coloured flowers. These have narrow segments and a long three-lobed lip.

In the wild, it grows in shady places in woodland often forming large dense colonies. It requires a sheltered shaded position in cultivation and grows best in a pot of compost D (see p. 27).

Figure 22
A, *Corybas dilatatus*; **B**, *C.fimbriatus*; **C**, *C.trilobus*

CYMBIDIUM

Cymbidium is the most popular and important of all orchid genera in cultivation. Most of the cymbidiums that are grown are hybrids bred over the past 100 years. The standard hybrids, which produce large long-lasting flowers for the buttonhole and sprays that can be bought from any florist, derive from a small number of large-flowered tropical and subtropical Himalayan and South-East Asian species such as *C.lowianum, C.tracyanum* and *C.insigne.* These vigorous plants will tolerate relatively low temperatures in winter and will survive outside with minimum protection in Mediterranean regions of the world. In the British Isles they can be placed out of doors in the early summer but they must be brought inside before the first frost of the autumn.

The miniature cymbidiums that are currently so popular as pot plants are if anything slightly hardier than the standard hybrids. Most derive from the hybridisation of standard hybrids with the Chinese species *C.floribundum* (syn. *C.pumilum*). Their dense spikes of relatively small brightly coloured flowers borne above the foliage of medium-sized plants make them ideal pot plants, and they are increasing rapidly in popularity.

Of the 46 species of *Cymbidium*, only a few are at all hardy. A complete account of the biology, taxonomy and cultivation of the genus has recently been published by Du Puy & Cribb (1988).

All can be grown in pots in compost A or C (see p. 26, 27). One or two are hardy enough to survive out of doors at Kew in woodland garden conditions.

C.faberi Rolfe
(FIGURE 23 B)

This is a terrestrial plant with small inconspicuous pseudobulbs and 5 to 9 slender linear grass-like leaves. It produces an erect spike, up to 60 cm tall, of 4 to 20 flowers. The green or yellowish sepals and petals are oblong-lanceolate to oblanceolate, and the three-lobed lip similarly coloured but purple-marked. *C.faberi* is closely allied to the widespread *C.ensifolium* but differs in having more

leaves and a lip with pronounced papillae on the surface of the mid-lobe.

It is a widespread species from Nepal and north India across China to Taiwan, growing on steep cliffs and slopes in open situations between 1,000 and 2,900 m (3,280–9,515 ft) elevation.

The Chinese and Japanese have cultivated it for centuries and many selected clones are now in cultivation there. It should be grown in the alpine house.

C.floribundum Lindley

This is the species better known in horticulture as *C.pumilum,* a later name. It is a lithophytic or rarely epiphytic species with small pseudobulbs up to 3 cm long, each bearing 5 to 6 linear leathery blunt leaves. The inflorescences are suberect and bear up to about 30 flowers in a dense cylindrical head. The 3 cm-wide flowers have purple or red-brown sepals and petals and a white lip spotted with red. The lip turns progressively redder as the flower ages. Albino forms are not uncommon in cultivation.

A widespread species from south-west China across to Taiwan, *C.floribundum* is found growing in the mountains, at altitudes up to 2,800 m (9,185 ft), in pine forests and on rocks either in open places or in partial shade.

C.floribundum has been an important influence in *Cymbidium* breeding since the last war. It has been crossed with large-flowered hybrids to produce the popular 'miniature' cymbidiums which are now sought after as pot plants. This is another subject for the warm end of the alpine house with a minimum temperature of 4–5°C (39–41°F).

C.goeringii Reichb.f.
(FIGURE 23 A)

C.goeringii could claim to have been in cultivation longer than any other species of orchid, having been grown by the Chinese for over 2,500 years and by the Japanese for several hundred. It is a variable species in the wild with three varieties currently being recognised. Two of these are common in cultivation and, over the centuries,

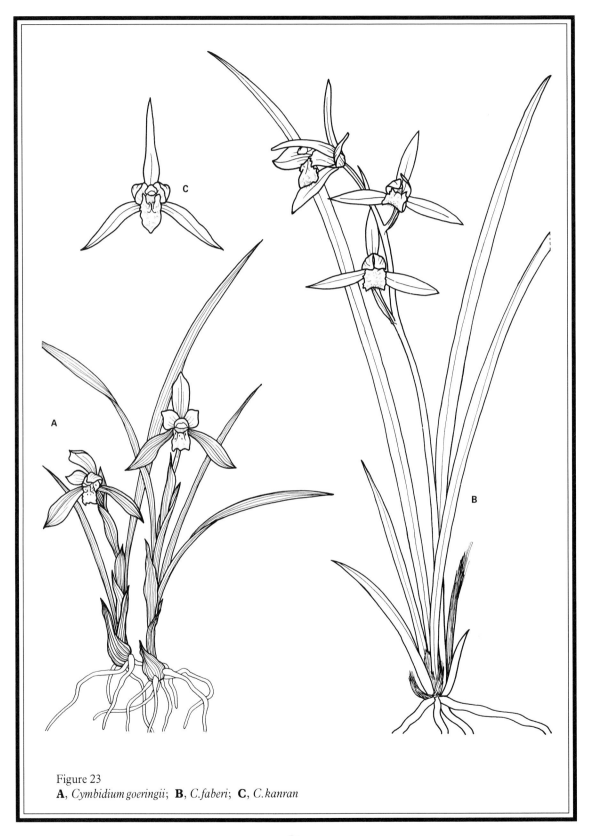

Figure 23
A, *Cymbidium goeringii*; **B**, *C.faberi*; **C**, *C.kanran*

many unusual forms of these which bear only a passing resemblance to the wild plants have been selected by growers. A complete account of the complex taxonomy of *C.goeringii* can be found in Du Puy & Cribb (1988).

The typical variety is a small plant with a small subterranean tuber-like pseudobulb which produces several slender dark green grass-like leaves. The solitary flower is borne at the apex of a 10–15 cm-tall erect stalk. The sepals and petals are green or yellow-green and the lip white and marked with purple spots. However, selected forms in cultivation with varying degrees of brown or orange on the sepals and petals and with variously shaped segments are common. Albino forms are much prized in Japan as are those with variegated leaves.

In the wild it grows in lightly shaded places on cliffs and slopes and often in coniferous woodland at the base of trees in deep leaf litter. At Kew, var.*goeringii* has been successfully grown for several years in a raised peat bed in a deep loam and leafmould compost, in a sheltered spot near the Alpine House. It flowers every year in April or May.

Var.*tortisepalum* (Fuk.)Wu & Chen differs from the typical variety in having two- or four-flowered inflorescences and shorter bracts. Its flowers have slenderer creamy rather than green sepals which usually have a twist in the middle. It has a more southerly distribution than var.*goeringii* and is known from western China and Taiwan. It is doubtfully hardy outside in the British Isles but is a suitable subject for the alpine house.

C.kanran Makino

(FIGURE 23C)

The spidery flowers of *C.kanran* make it the most distinctive of the terrestrial species allied to *C.goeringii*, *C.ensifolium* and *C.sinense*. It has narrowly ovoid pseudobulbs which each bear 3 to 5 linear grass-like leaves and, from the base, an erect 5- to 12-flowered inflorescence up to 60 cm tall. The flowers are strongly scented and have distinctive linear tapering sepals and petals that are usually apple-green or olive-green. The three-lobed lip is pale yellow to pale green and marked with red.

It is another of the widespread Asiatic species found from south-west China across to Taiwan and north to Korea and southern Japan. It grows in open hardwood forest in shade in deep leaf litter at between 800 and 1,800 m (2,625–5,905 ft) elevation.

CYPRIPEDIUM

Few plants excite more admiration and the collector's lust than the Lady's Slipper Orchids. The native British species, *C.calceolus*, is alas also the rarest, reduced nowadays, as previously mentioned, to a single plant in its only remaining locality in the north of England. It has become a symbol of what might happen to indigenous British species if they are not given the protection they deserve.

Reginald Farrer as long ago as 1908 wrote 'wickednesses untold have been perpetrated upon this plant'. Even in those days the surviving plants in the known colonies were deflowered each year to prevent their being seen and dug up or picked by the ignorant or unscrupulous. Nevertheless, collectors, both botanical and horticultural, have exterminated it from all of its known localities bar one. There, a single plant has lingered for over 40 years, a reminder of the unthinking depredations of our forefathers, a treasure that has almost slipped away.

On the Continent, it is also under threat but many of its choicer habitats are now protected as nature reserves. Nevertheless, it is still dug up in some quantity and specimens of eastern European origin have in recent years been offered for sale as bare root plants. These are very difficult to establish and usually die a lingering death in the garden. It must also be said that it is most unlikely that these plants would nowadays be on sale legally.

A few *Cypripedium* species are still offered for sale in small quantities in the British Isles and on the Continent. These are species from either North America or Asia. Darnell (1930) listed 42 species in his account *Orchids in the Outdoor Garden*. However, less than half of these have ever been seen in cultivation. At the present time, we doubt if more than ten species could be found in trade in the British Isles, since most species are protected in their native countries. However, a few have been successfully propagated both vegetatively and from seed and these may well appear in trade in increasing numbers over the next few years.

Case (1987) has successfully grown many of the North American species out of doors in a slightly acid to neutral loam, or even garden soil if not fertilised. The artificial bog methods of Whitlow and Holman are dealt with on pages 17–19, and cultivation in containers can be found on page 31.

The following species have all proved hardy in the British Isles.

C.acaule Aiton

(FIGURE 24A)

This is the commonest of the North American slipper orchids and has the delightful popular name of Moccasin Flower, from its unusual inflated lip.

Two large elliptic leaves are produced at ground level to cup the base of the flower stalk. The solitary flower has maroon sepals and petals but it is dominated by the large inflated rose-purple pouched lip. The lip is distinctively pleated in front. An albino form with a white lip is occasionally seen in the wild.

C.acaule was one of the first of the slipper orchids to be grown in the British Isles, and was figured in *Curtis's Botanical Magazine* (t.192) in 1792. It is, however, one of the trickier species in cultivation and will often flower well the first year but not reappear the following spring. This may be because the plants are sold bare rooted and the absence of the fungal symbiont is detrimental to the plant. It is widespread and locally common in many north-eastern and eastern seaboard states of the United States and also in eastern and central Canada. In the wild it grows in the higher and drier parts of coniferous woods, often in a thin layer of pine needles over rocks. It is also found growing in bogs in some places.

C.arietinum R.Br.

This is one of the least attractive but most readily distinguished of the hardy slipper orchids. It is a softly pubescent plant up to 30 cm tall with three to four elliptic spreading pleated leaves in the middle part of the stem. The solitary flower is rather small, 3–4 cm long with distinctive narrow deflexed lateral sepals and petals and a characteristic pouched, white and purplish lip that comes to a somewhat reflexed conical point at the base. The fanciful resemblance of the flower to the head of a ram has given it the common name "Ram's-head slipper orchid" in North America.

In the wild it grows in sphagnum bogs with Thuja but also in shady places on thin dry soils over limestone or beach sand. It is a rare species although it can be locally abundant. Its range extends from coastal NE USA and adjacent Canada westwards to the Great Lakes and Manitoba.

C.calceolus L.

The Lady's Slipper Orchid is the most widespread species in the genus, with the typical variety ranging throughout Europe and temperate Asia and three distinct varieties in North America.

The typical variety is a plant of calcareous woods and pastures up to 2,000 m (6,560 ft) in the Alps. it has dark maroon- or rarely cinnamon-coloured sepals and petals and a bright yellow lip. The oblong concave staminode is also yellow but has red spotting down each side. One to three flowers can be borne on each stalk. Well-grown plants of many growths and flowers can be sometimes seen both in the wild and in cultivation. However, such large plants are unusual and most plants will have from 1 to 10 shoots.

This variety is successfully grown in the British Isles in a compost of leafmould derived from conifer needles and beech leaves with added grit and limestone chips. It does not like peat in the mix, unlike the next variety. We have seen large colonies successfully grown in both full sun on a rock garden and also in partial shade under beech and conifers. Once established a plant can be expected to live for many years if a regular mulch of leafmould is applied.

Figure 24
A, *Cypripedium acaule*; **B**, *C. reginae*; **C**, *C. calceolus* var. *pubescens*

The best known of the North American varieties is var.*pubescens* (Figure 24C, p. 79). It is similar to the typical variety but differs in having generally densely pubescent leaves, one or two rather larger flowers, longer greenish or pale brown petals and a yellow unspotted staminode. It seems to be far more tolerant in its habitat preference than the other varieties, and is found in both forests and pastures from the plains to the mountains where it can be found in flower as late as August. It is widespread and locally common in the eastern United States and Canada but rarer in the West.

Var.*pubescens* can be successfully grown in compost D (see p. 27) or one of equal parts of peat and leafmould to which some grit has been added to improve the drainage. In North America its hairy leaves have a reputation, similar to Poison Ivy, for irritating the skin of some people.

Of the North American varieties, var.*parviflorum* resembles the typical variety most closely. However, the plants are daintier, the flowers smaller and the plants less pubescent. Furthermore, the habitat of this variety is rather distinct. It grows in full sun in wet bogs and swamps. It is not uncommon in the north-eastern United States and adjacent Canada where it flowers in May and June. This variety is an ideal subject for the bog garden and should be planted in a peaty mix.

The last of the North American varieties, var.*planipetalum*, is also the rarest, confined to the far north-east where it grows in shallow grassy depressions in the treeless limestone tundra. It is the shortest of the varieties rarely reaching 20 cm tall with it leaves clustered towards the base of the stem. A solitary flower or rarely two are borne at the apex of the stem. The sepals and petals are characteristically yellowish-green and the latter are flat and untwisted. The staminode is also plain yellow and unspotted.

The recently described *C.kentuckiense* from the southern USA is very closely allied to var. *pubescens* but has larger flowers with rusty-brown sepals and petals and a larger lip.

C.californicum A.Gray

This rare orchid has proved surprisingly hardy in the British Isles. It can produce clumps of many stems that reach a metre or more tall in the most favourable conditions. Five to ten elliptic pleated leaves are borne along the stems which can bear 4 to 12 flowers in their apical half. The flowers are small, up to 3.5 cm across, but the pure white lip and hairy yellow-green sepals and petals produce a charming effect.

C.californicum has a restricted distribution in the mountains of northern California and southern Oregon and is a local or rare plant throughout its range. It grows by springs and along rocky streams, in partial shade in coniferous forest, and often with the strange pitcher plant, *Darlingtonia californica.*

This species will thrive in a raised peat bed to which a generous amount of leafmould has been added, together with some grit to assist drainage.

C.candidum Willd.

This rare orchid is closely allied to *C.calceolus* but differs in having a single flower, about the same size as that of var.*parviflorum*, which has green sepals and petals, sometimes flushed with brown, and a white lip. It is confined to the north-eastern part of North America where it grows in moist meadows.

It can be grown in a similar way to var.*parviflorum* and should be given light shade.

C.cordigerum D.Don
(FIGURE 25C)

This is one of several Himalayan species that are occasionally brought into cultivation in the British Isles. It looks rather like *C.calceolus* and *C.montanum* in its habit and in the shape and size of its flowers, but the sepals and petals are green and the lip white with orange hairs within. Well-grown specimens will form a clump which produces inflorescences bearing a single flower with a 10 cm spread.

In the wild, it grows in lightly shaded places up to 3,500 m (11,480 ft) altitude. In cultivation it also prefers a shady spot and should be grown in deep calcareous loam with added leafmould or chopped decomposing beech or oak leaves.

C.debile Reichb.f.

(FIGURE 25B)

A dainty species that has appeared with increasing frequency in trade over the past few years. Farrer (1908) was too harsh in his disdain of it as 'conspicuous only for its extreme inconspicuousness and a flopping debility entitling it to the name it bears'. In reality it has an undeniable charm, the plant resembling the Lesser Twayblade in habit with the small flower nodding beneath the opposite leaves. The flowers have pale green sepals and petals and a white lip lightly spotted with purple.

It grows well in a pot in an alpine house where it can be seen to its best advantage. 'Euphrasia', in the *Bulletin of the Alpine Garden Society* (1988), reported that *C.debile* 'planted in cracks of a mossed-over piece of bark, was an elegant revelation'; altogether an unusual and imaginative method.

C.guttatum Sw.

A widespread species from the Urals to northern Japan and in North America in Alaska and northwestern Canada, *C.guttatum* is one of the smaller species growing up to 25 cm tall. It has two basal ascending pubescent leaves and a one-flowered inflorescence. The fleshy flower has very narrow short petals, less than 2 cm long and 8 mm wide, and a pitcher-like lip 1.8 to 2.2 cm long. The flowers are white flushed with purple or brown on the dorsal sepal and heavily spotted with purple or brownish-purple on the petals and lip. The staminode can be yellow or white and is sometimes spotted with purple on the margins.

It grows in meadows and woods, and in Alaska grows in open birch woods on hillsides in association with the Dwarf Cornel. *Cornus canadensis.*

Var.*yatabeanum* replaces the typical variety in Japan and the Aleutian Islands. It differs in having larger leaves and flowers and spathulate petals. Both varieties flower in June and July in the wild.

C.henryi Rolfe

Although one of the less attractive species.

C.henryi is nowadays not uncommon in cultivation. It is rather like a small *C.calceolus* but with green sepals and petals, the latter being untwisted. The lip and staminode are like smaller versions of those of *C.calceolus*, although occasionally the lip can be spotted with red.

C.henryi is a native of China where it is widespread from NW Yunnan, Sichuan, Gansu, S.Shansi and E.Hubei, growing from 800–2300 m altitude. It flowers in April and May in the wild and in cultivation.

C.japonicum Thunb.

This is an elegant species that vies with *C.reginae* as the finest of the genus. In form it is elegant, and the paired fishtail leaves have an exotic air that sets it apart in this marvellous genus. Two varieties are known: the typical one (Figure 25A, p.82) is found in Japan and China; while var.*formosanum* is endemic to Taiwan.

Most of the cultivated material of the typical variety has come in recent years from Japan rather than China, but the alarming flood of wild-collected material from China recently may well change that. It is a pity because *C.japonicum* is widely cultivated and propagated in Japan and there is no need for it to be stripped from the wild.

This orchid is eye-catching whether in flower or not. The paired pleated fan-shaped leaves are borne at the top of a short pubescent stalk. The flower, carried well clear of the leaves on a slender stalk, can reach 10 cm across. its sepals and petals are pale green lightly spotted at the base with pink. The white-and-pink-mottled lip is large and has a distinctive corrugated apical margin.

In nature it grows in lightly shaded woods in deep leaf litter, often forming large colonies. It prefers a woodland mix, and should be given lightly shaded and frost-free conditions.

The Taiwanese variety, var.*formosanum*, is usually traded as *C.formosanum*. Its habit is the same as that of the typical variety but it differs in having pale pink sepals and petals, the latter rather broader, a much less hairy ovary and a somewhat apiculate apex to the lip. It is found growing at between 2,200 and 2,900 m (9,515 ft) in nature. In cultivation it should be given similar

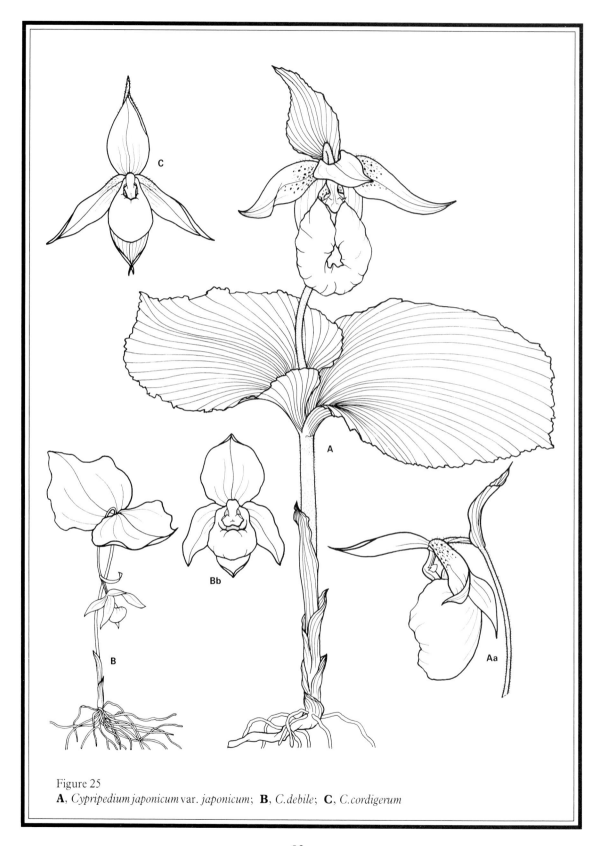

Figure 25
A, *Cypripedium japonicum* var. *japonicum*; **B**, *C.debile*; **C**, *C.cordigerum*

treatment to var.*japonicum*. Both will also grow well in clay pots in an open compost of chopped leaves or leafmould, bark chips, charcoal and chopped *Sphagnum* moss. Sadly this variety has been dug up in quantity from the wild and its export continues on a large scale even now.

C.macranthum Sw.

(FIGURE 26A)

This is one of the most widespread and also one of the most variable of the slipper orchids with a distribution stretching from European Russia to Japan. Most of the plants in cultivation come from Japan but Chinese plants have recently appeared in trade in increasing numbers.

The habit of *C.macranthum* is rather like that of *C.calceolus* but it is usually a more robust plant, 30–45 cm tall, with several broad pleated downy leaves along the stem. One or rarely two large flowers up to 8 cm across are borne at the apex of the stem. These are usually deep purple and somewhat checkered on the lip. However, salmon-pink- and white-flowered forms are popular in cultivation. The lip of *C.macranthum* is particularly impressive and, with its broad sepals and petals, give the flower a solid look.

In nature it grows on the margins and in clearings in woodland, in light stony soils, and in rocky scree in the mountains up to 3,500 m (11,480 ft) elevation. Reginald Farrer, who saw it in the wild in Japan on Mt Fujiyama, ecstatically described it as 'far away above *C.reginae*', praise indeed. It is probably one of the hardiest species in the genus and has survived several hard winters outside at Kew, on a peat bed in a sheltered and partly shaded spot. It prefers a compost of rich loam and leafmould with added grit for sharp drainage.

The Himalayan and Chinese species *C.tibeticum* is closely related, but is a shorter plant with a larger dark purple lip with broader basal lobes and a corrugated surface.

C.margaritaceum Franch.

(FIGURE 26B)

This is certainly the most distinctive species in the genus, immediately recognisable by its large paired prostrate leaves, up to 20 cm long and 18 cm wide, that are spotted with blackish-maroon. It is the only *Cypripedium* with spotted leaves. The solitary flower is also unusual, nestling between the leaves on a short stalk. The sepals are yellow or greenish-yellow, sometimes maroon-flecked, and deeply concave, the dorsal being prominent above the flower. The petals are unique in the genus in clasping the lip on either side. They are pubescent, yellow and heavily spotted with maroon. The lip, distinguished by its very small mouth, points forward and is also yellow and spotted with maroon around its rim. The staminode is large and also heavily spotted with maroon.

It is found in south-western China in the provinces of Yunnan, Sichuan and Hupeh, where it grows amongst rocks in pine woods in partial shade from 2,400 to 3,800 m (7,875–12,470 ft). It has been introduced into cultivation several times this century and has recently appeared in some quantity in Europe via Japan. A recent report of its successful cultivation is given by Kohls (1988) in the journal *Die Orchidee*.

C.montanum Douglas ex Lindley

In the mountains of north-western North America, *C.montanum* replaces the closely allied *C.calceolus*. It differs from that species in the colour of its flowers which have a pure white lip and deep maroon sepals and petals. Each stem can have from 1 to 3 of these striking flowers.

In the wild it grows happily in almost full sun in dry scrubby woodland, as well as in full shade of wet coniferous forests in valleys such as in the Yosemite National Park. In cultivation it should be treated in the same way as *C.calceolus* var.*pubescens*.

C.reginae Walter

(FIGURE 24B)

The most splendid of all the North American species is undoubtedly the Queen Lady's Slipper Orchid, *C.reginae*. It can produce sizeable clumps of many stems, each 30–100 cm tall, with from 1 to 4 flowers on each. The flowers have white

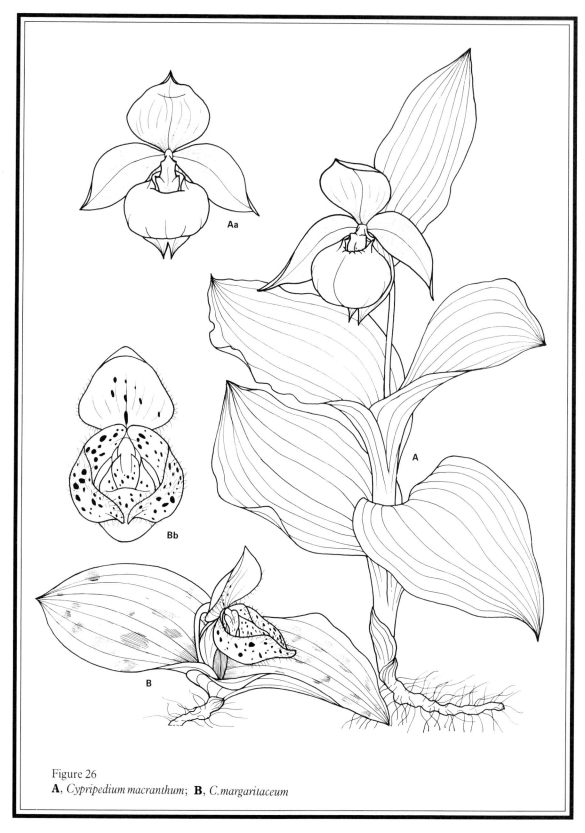

Figure 26
A, *Cypripedium macranthum*; **B**, *C.margaritaceum*

sepals and petals, a pink lip with a paler margin and a white staminode flushed with yellow on the margins and spotted with red towards the centre. Plants with pure white flowers are rarely seen in the wild.

Cypripedium reginae is not uncommon in northern and eastern North America across to the Great Lakes where it typically grows on or near the margins of bogs. The Royal Fern, *Osmunda regalis*, is commonly associated with *C.reginae*; a wonderful regal twosome! Even where it grows in acid *Sphagnum* bogs it usually has its roots deep down in almost neutral conditions.

Once established in cultivation, *C.reginae* will grow to form a large clump. The largest we have seen are in the Geneva Botanic Garden where two clumps on the rock garden in full sun produce over 50 flowers each year in early June. It is more frequently seen planted in a cool shadier place in a compost of peat, leafmould and loam mixed with gritty sand. Reginald Farrer's recommendation that 'no one with a bog garden can ignore this glorious plant, so thrifty and hardy, with its handsome tall leafy stems and its roundish flowers of pure white and rose, in June and early July' cannot be bettered.

The Chinese species *C.flavum* is closely related but differs in having pale yellow flowers.

DACTYLORHIZA

Dactylorhizas, variously called marsh or spotted orchids, are amongst the most vigorous, desirable and readily available of all orchids for the garden. For many years dactylorhizas were included in the genus *Orchis* but it is now widely accepted that their floral similarities are not indicative of a particularly close relationship. Their most obvious distinctions from *Orchis* lie in their tubers which are divided into tapering segments, and their bracts which are prominent and surpass the flowers in length. Unfortunately, considerable confusion persists in the nursery trade where they are still frequently sold as *Orchis* species. In our experience most of those in commerce are also misidentified. This is not surprising because the genus is a nightmare for the taxonomist and the distinctions between many of the species are

blurred. Furthermore, the sympatric species frequently hybridise in nature and also in cultivation. The hybrids exhibit a degree of hybrid vigour that has led to several being selected by gardeners, and these have become rather widespread in cultivation as a result.

Baumann and Künkele (1982), in their account of European and Middle Eastern orchids, have recognised 24 species of which six are native to the British Isles. The genus is, however, widely distributed through temperate Asia and a single species, *D.aristata*, reaches North America. Of the native British species, the Southern Marsh Orchid, *D.praetermissa*, and the Northern Marsh Orchid. *D.purpurella*, are the most gardenworthy. In Cedric Morris's famous garden in Hadleigh, Suffolk, we saw both of these and some vigorous hybrids growing rampantly all over the beds. To label all of the species as marsh orchids is misleading. The Common Spotted Orchid, *D.fuchsii*, is the commonest British chalk grassland species and many of the others will grow quite happily in a variety of soil types.

Without doubt two species, the Madeiran Orchid, *D.foliosa*, and the South-west European and North African species *D.elata*, stand literally head and shoulders above the others. These stately vividly coloured orchids can grow to a metre or more tall and form impressive clumps in suitable situations.

D.elata (Poir.)Soó
(FIGURE 27C)

Well-grown plants of this superb orchid can surpass a metre in height, and the cylindrical dense spikes of bright magenta flowers remind us of those of Purple Loosestrife from a distance. This species can have either unspotted or, less commonly, spotted leaves. It is closely related to *D.praetermissa* which replaces it in north-western Europe, but it differs in usually being a much taller-growing plant and in having more vivid dark magenta flowers. It is also commonly confused with *D.foliosa* but differs in being a slender plant with shorter narrower leaves and in having a narrower less markedly three-lobed lip, strongly marked with dark purple streaks and with strongly reflexed side lobes. The lateral sepals also stand erect or reflexed, reminding one strongly of a bird in flight.

Dactylorhiza elata is widespread in south-western Europe from western and southern France, Corsica and Sicily to southern Spain, and also in North Africa. In the Atlas Mountains it is found up to 2,200 m (7,220 ft) altitude.

In the wild it grows in water seepages and marshy areas and amongst grasses in wet meadows, usually in full sun. In cultivation it thrives in compost D (see p.27), kept moist throughout the growing season.

D.foliosa (Verm.)Soó
(FIGURE 27A)

Although endemic to the island of Madeira, *D.foliosa* is quite hardy in the British Isles, appreciating no doubt the cool mild summer weather. It is occasionally sold as *Orchis maderensis*, a later synonym.

In cultivation outside it usually grows 50 to 70 cm tall, but in a protected spot will sometimes grow taller. In suitable conditions it will produce large clumps, with vigorous plants doubling or even trebling their size each season. Its growth habit is a little cabbagy with several large spreading glossy unspotted leaves borne along each stem. These bear dense 5 to 15 cm-long heads of purple or magenta large flowers, which are characterised by their broad strongly three-lobed lip and forward spreading short broad sepals and petals. The lip is also concolorous or only weakly marked with faint lines.

Many of the plants sold as *D.foliosa* are, in fact, *D.elata* or even *D.praetermissa*. The differences are noted in the relevant accounts of these species.

D.foliosa is sometimes seen in displays at the Royal Horticultural Society's shows. A particularly memorable display of a large group was presented by the Royal Parks at a recent Chelsea Flower Show. At Kew a large clump forms the centrepiece of the June display in the new pyramidal Alpine House.

One of the most striking hybrids that we have seen was a plant of *D.foliosa* crossed with *D.majalis*, cultivated at the Royal Botanic Garden in Edinburgh. It was a large plant, about 70 cm tall, with spotted leaves, and flowers with a large broad lip of vivid magenta and with bold darker streaks on its surface.

D.fuchsii (Druce)Soó
(FIGURE 28A)

This, the Common Spotted Orchid, is the commonest of the native British species, widespread in neutral and calcareous grassland. It grows to about 35 cm tall and has leaves with bold spots on their upper surface. The flowers are borne in a dense head that is markedly pyramidal in shape but becomes cylindrical as it develops. The flowers are usually pale pink, streaked on the lip with dark purple. The lip is strongly three-lobed, with the mid-lobe slightly longer than the side lobes. It is often confused in Britain with the Heath Spotted Orchid, *D.maculata* subsp.*ericetorum*, but that has a lip that is weakly three-lobed and fan-shaped, with the side lobes larger than the small mid-lobe.

This species will grow well in most garden soils but prefers an open compost of loam, leafmould and gritty sand. Limestone or dolomite chips can be added and may encourage seedlings to grow. It should be placed in a sunny or lightly shaded place where it is not crowded by the surrounding vegetation.

D.maculata (L.)Soó

The Heath Spotted Orchid replaces the Common Spotted in acidic soils in the British Isles. This is a species with several subspecies throughout its range; all of the British plants are referable to subsp.*ericetorum* (Figure 28C, p.89) which is readily distinguished by its spotted leaves, pale pink flowers lightly spotted with purple on the lip, and the lip which is weakly three-lobed with rounded side lobes and a small mid-lobe that is usually shorter than the side lobes.

In the British Isles, it hybridises rather frequently with most of the other species. These are usually intermediate between their parents in flower colour and shape, but can be vigorous plants, larger than their respective parents.

Figure 27
A, *Dactylorhiza foliosa*; **B**, *D.praetermissa*; **C**, *D.elata*

On the Continent, *D.maculata* occurs in many named subspecies, varieties and forms which are generally characterised by their spotted leaves and pink or pale purple flowers spotted with purple.

Like the Common Spotted Orchid, it is an easy subject in cultivation and will thrive in most gardens with the minimum of fuss. It will tolerate shaded positions much better than most of the other species.

D.majalis (Reichb.f.)Hunt & Summerh.

This is also known as *D.latifolia* (or *Orchis latifolia*). It is a rare plant in the British Isles, found only in a few places in Ireland, Scotland and Wales, but it is widespread on the Continent where it is particularly common in bogs, marshes and wet flushes in the mountains of central Europe, such as the Alps and Jura, at altitudes up to 2,600 m (8,530 ft).

It usually has spotted leaves and dark purple flowers spotted with dark purple on the lip. The three-lobed lip has a mid-lobe that extends beyond the spreading side lobes.

D.praetermissa (Druce)Soó
(FIGURE 27B)

The Southern Marsh Orchid is the largest British species and probably the most gardenworthy. It is usually 30–50 cm tall but can reach 80 cm tall in favourable habitats. It has unspotted leaves with a somewhat hooded tip and pale purple flowers with fine darker spots on the lip. The flowers are distinguished by their obscurely three-lobed or even unlobed lip in which the mid-lobe is longer than the side lobes.

It grows, as its common name suggests, in marshes and wet meadows where it can form sizeable colonies. In cultivation it prefers a peaty compost with added leafmould and should be kept moist throughout the growing season. Fine colonies can be seen growing by a small stream in the rock garden at Kew.

D. × grandis (Druce)Hunt, the hybrid of this species with *D.maculata*, is one of the most attractive of the *Dactylorhiza* hybrids. It occurs naturally in southern and central England and on the Continent and is not infrequent in cultivation. Well-grown plants can reach 70 cm tall and are topped with a splendid spike, up to 20 cm long, of deep pinkish-purple flower. Plants usually have spotted leaves. In the UK, fine clumps of this can be seen at Sissinghurst, Kent.

D.purpurella (T. & T.A. Stephenson)Soó
(FIGURE 28B)

The Northern Marsh Orchid is rather like a small version of its southern relative, differing in its smaller blunter leaves and smaller deep purple flowers in which the lip is often almost rhombic and unlobed.

It grows in meadows and marshy ground throughout the northern parts of the British Isles, the Orkneys and Shetlands and in coastal parts of Scandinavia. In cultivation it should be kept moist throughout the growing season.

DACTYLOSTALIX

A monotypic genus endemic to Japan and closely allied to *Calypso*.

D.ringens Reichb.f.
(FIGURE 18B)

This pretty dwarf species resembles *Calypso bulbosa* in its habit, producing a single pleated leaf at the base and an elongate inflorescence, up to 15 cm tall, from its underground rhizome. The inflorescence is one-flowered at the apex and the flower is about 2 cm across. The sepals and petals are yellowish-green and the reflexed three-lobed lip, white and spotted with purple.

It is best grown in a pot in the alpine house where its subtle charm can be best appreciated and the grower can control appreciative slugs and snails. It should be grown in a peaty compost with added leafmould and grit and be placed in a shaded place.

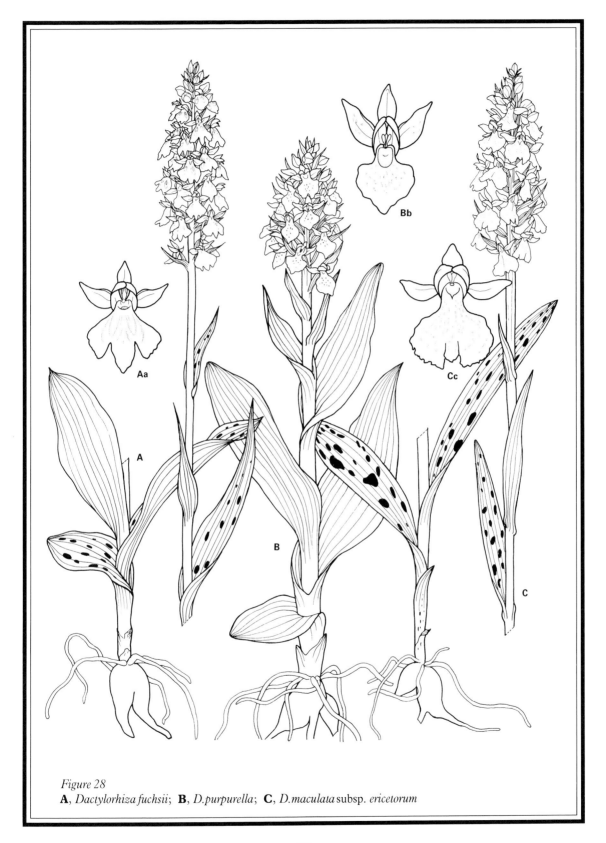

Figure 28
A, *Dactylorhiza fuchsii*; **B**, *D.purpurella*; **C**, *D.maculata* subsp. *ericetorum*

DENDROBIUM

Readers may be surprised to see the predominantly tropical and subtropical genus *Dendrobium* included here. However, of the 1,000 or so species, one at least is hardy in the south-west of the British Isles but will require an alpine house elsewhere. Use compost A (see p. 26).

D.moniliforme (L.)Sw
(FIGURE 29A)

This dainty epiphyte is widespread in China and in Japan as far north as the Tokyo area. It usually produces clusters of stems of several nodes from 5 to 20 cm long which have lanceolate, somewhat leathery leaves in their upper part. One to several inflorescences are produced from the upper nodes, each bearing one or two flowers. The flowers are white, rarely shaded with pale pink on the sepals, with a few purple spots at the base of the lip.

In most of the British Isles, *D.moniliforme* can be grown in a frost-free greenhouse. The displays of this attractive orchid at the World Orchid Conference Show in Tokyo and Hiroshima in March 1987 were a revelation, wonderfully enhancing the displays of native orchids.

DISA

The genus *Disa* contains some of the most spectacular African terrestrial orchids. It is a genus of about 120 species, mostly South African but with a number of species in East Africa, as far north as Ethiopia, and also with a few species in Madagascar. The genus is distinguished by the hooded and spurred dorsal sepal, spreading lateral sepals, small petal adnate to the dorsal sepal, the small entire lip and the erect or recumbent column.

Despite the showy flowers of many species few are in cultivation. However, the spectacular *D.uniflora* and its now numerous hybrids are a glorious exception. This orchid, the Pride of Table Mountain, has proved easy to grow in pot-culture and it has been used to produce a range of hybrids from its flower size and colour. The orchids can be grown in a variety of composts from washed sand or living *Sphagnum* to compost F (see p. 27).

D.tripetaloides (L.f.)N.E.Br.

This is a slender species that will grow to 60 cm tall. It has narrowly lanceolate leaves and a lax spike of many white or pink flowers, 1.4 to 3.2 cm across. The rare subspecies *aurata* has bright yellow flowers.

The horticultural significance of *D.tripetaloides* lies in its ability to cross with *D.uniflora* to produce some remarkable hybrids. It figures in the ancestry of most *Disa* hybrids such as *D.Kewensis*, *D.Watsonii* and *D.Diores*.

D.tripetaloides is a widespread species in the Cape, Natal and Transkei growing on the banks of streams and on damp mountain slopes from sea-level to 1,000 m (3,280 ft). It grows well in pots in a sandy compost that is kept moist during the growing season.

D.uniflora Berg.

This wonderful orchid is now a common species in cultivation and has almost lost its reputation for being difficult to grow. In the composts used nowadays it grows vigorously and multiplies freely. The plant grows to 60 cm tall and has one or rarely two large flowers, 7 to 12 cm across. The flowers have orange-red lateral sepals and a yellow dorsal sepal strongly veined with dark orange-red. Around Worcester in the Cape this species has rose-pink flowers while a pure yellow-flowered form has been very rarely seen in the wild. *D.uniflora* is confined to the western Cape, where it grows in full sun or in half or full shade by streams and in seepages between 100 and 1,200 m (328–3,935 ft).

In cultivation this species requires minimum temperatures of 4–5 (39–41°F).

DIURIS

Diuris is a genus of about 26 species of which all but one are endemic to Australia where they are commonly called Donkey Orchids because of their prominent erect ear-like petals. They are terrestrial orchids which grow from ovoid or elongate underground tubers. The inflorescences are usually laxly-flowered bearing a few showy

Figure 29
A, *Dendrobium moniliforme*; **B**, *Cremastra appendiculata*

flowers. The flowers have prominent spathulate petals, parallel narrow pendent lateral sepals and a three-lobed lip with a convex mid-lobe.

They are usually easy to grow in pots in the warmer section of a frost-free glasshouse, in a free-draining compost of gritty sand, leafmould and wood chips (compost E, p.27). The plants need to be watered well during the growing season. Repotting should be undertaken every two or three years when the tubers are dormant. They should be planted 3 to 4 cm deep, and not watered until the new shoot has started to grow. A full account of *Diuris* in cultivation is given by Elliot & Jones (1984).

There are several vigorous and free-flowering hybrids in cultivation in Australia which may be worth trying. The first of these was *D.Pioneer*, a hybrid of *D.maculata* and *D.longifolia.*

D.aurea J.E.Smith

A colony-forming species, *D.aurea* produces two basal linear channelled leaves, 3 to 6 mm wide, and a 2- to 5-flowered inflorescence 15 to 50 cm tall. The flowers are deep golden-yellow to orange-yellow, occasionally with a few brown markings. The lip is prominent and has a large mid-lobe.

It is a locally common plant in eastern Australia as far south as Sydney and grows in open forest.

D.longifolia Lindl.
(FIGURE 30B)

This is the commonest and most widespread of the Australian species and also one of the handsomest. It has one to three basal linear deeply channelled leaves, and an inflorescence of 1 to 8 flowers that can reach 50 cm in height. The flowers are rather variable in size, from 2.5 to 5 cm across, and also in colour ranging from clear yellow to brownish-yellow and marked with mauve. The side lobes of the lip are as large as the mid-lobe.

It grows mainly in open forest and in heathland where its flowering is markedly stimulated by bush fires. In cultivation it multiplies freely but can be a shy flowerer needing some stimulation to produce a good show.

D.maculata J.E.Smith
(FIGURE 30A)

A slighter plant than the previous one, this species will grow 15 to 35 cm tall and produces 2 to 8 smaller flowers on a flexuous stalk. The 1.5 to 3 cm-wide flowers are attractively blotched with dark brown on a bright yellow background.

It is a common and widespread orchid in eastern and south-eastern Australia as far north as New South Wales, growing in scattered colonies in scrub, forest and in rocky places. It was first flowered in Britain in 1810 and is one of the species that will grow and flower readily in cultivation there.

D.punctata J.E.Smith

Not all of the *Diuris* have yellow flowers. This species has purple or lilac flowers and is one of the most attractive in the genus. It can produce an inflorescence from 30 to 60 cm tall, carrying 2 to 8 flowers on its stout stalk. The flowers can vary from 3 to 8 cm across and some forms have very long lateral sepals extending several cm below the lip.

It is widespread in eastern Australia and sometimes locally common, although var. *albo-violacea* from around Melbourne is now on the verge of extinction. It can be grown easily in pots where it flowers freely.

ELEORCHIS

A monotypic genus that is rarely seen in cultivation in Europe but more frequently in Japan, where the native endemic *E.japonica* is prized.

E.japonica (Gray)Maekwa
(FIGURE 18A)

In its habit, this dwarf species resembles *Arethusa* or a dwarf *Bletilla*. In the spring, a single erect leaf and a terminal inflorescence are produced from a small ovoid to conical but tiny pseudobulb. The flower is about 2 cm long and borne at the apex of a slender stalk up to 25 cm long. The suberect flower is narrow and rose-purple or pink.

Figure 30
A, *Diuris maculata*; **B**, *D. longifolia*

In the wild, it grows in swampy places and marshes. In cultivation, it probably needs a pot but will survive in a well-protected spot in a peat bed. It should be grown in compost D (see p. 27) and should be kept moist during the growing season.

EPIPACTIS

The genus *Epipactis* is widespread in Europe where some 15 species are found. However, the genus spreads across Asia to the Far East, with two species native to Japan, and to North America where there is one native and one introduced species. They are known as Helleborines but should not be confused with the similarly named species of *Cephalanthera*.

Two species, *E.gigantea* and *E.palustris*, are in our view among the best of all orchids for the garden while some of the others, such as the Broad-leaved Helleborine, *E.helleborine*, appears quite often in gardens, especially under old hedges and by ditches.

E.atrorubens (Hoffm.)Besser.
(FIGURE 31C)

The Dark-red Helleborine is a native species with a widespread but patchy distribution across Europe as far as the Caucasus. It can be a sturdy plant 20 to 70 cm tall with 5 to 10 leaves, that are often red-tinged, borne along the pubescent reddish stem. The flowers are usually dark red or purple and 7 to 10 mm across. The lip is short, only 5.5–6.5 mm long, and is recurved at the tip.

It is a plant of limestone districts where it grows amongst rocks and on screes in full sun or in partial shade. It is essentially a plant of mountainous areas up to 2,200 m (7,220 ft) elevation and flowering from May until August. It should be grown in compost C (see p. 27) with added limestone chips.

E.gigantea Douglas ex Hooker
(FIGURE 31A)

The only native North American species in the genus, *E.gigantea* is also the most amenable species in cultivation. In the garden it usually grows 30–50 cm tall, but in suitable conditions can reach a metre in height. It has 4–15 pleated pubescent leaves along the stem with a terminal inflorescence of 5 to 15 flowers, each subtended and overtopped by a leafy bract. The flowers are yellowish or greenish, flushed with purple on the sepals and veined with brownish-purple on the broad petals and lip side lobes. The mid-lobe of the lip is white with a fleshy chestnut-brown and yellow bilobed callus at the base. Its flowers are not unlike those of *E.veratrifolia*, a widespread species in the Middle East, Arabia and Ethiopia across to the Himalaya.

In the wild it grows in moist places along the gravelly or sandy shores of streams and even in the stream bed in shallow water, often in full sun. It will survive complete inundation there. It is also found in seepages on shaded banks and in salty soils by hot springs. In cultivation it will grow in a variety of situations. At Kew a large colony thrives beside a small stream in the rock garden where it grows in a loam, peat and leafmould compost in partial shade, a position it shares with *Caltha palustris*, dactylorhizas and Skunk Cabbage (*Lysichiton camtschatcense*). A similar large colony can also be found growing in the Geneva Botanic Garden on their rock garden in a far drier and sunnier spot next to their fine clumps of *Cypripedium reginae*.

E.palustris (L.)Crantz
(FIGURE 31B)

The Marsh Helleborine is the prettiest species in the genus and will thrive in cultivation in moist places. Plants vary from 25 to 60 cm tall but will reach 70 cm in favourable conditions. Like all *Epipactis*, the leaves and stems are densely shortly pubescent but the leaves are narrow, 2.5–4 cm wide. The inflorescence is 6–20 cm long and 5–15-flowered. The flowers are nodding and have yellow sepals veined with purplish-red, whitish petals with a red-flushed base and a white lip with red-veined side lobes, and a yellow-tipped callus at the base of the apical lobe.

It is widespread but local in the British Isles, where it grows in damp grassland and marshes in

Figure 31
A, *Epipactis gigantea*; **B**, *E. palustris*; **C**, *E. atrorubens*

calcareous or neutral soils. On the Continent, it is found in similar situations and also in wet flushes on hillsides up to 2,000 m (6,560 ft).

In cultivation, *E.palustris* is relatively tolerant and thrives in sunny places in a loamy soil with added leaf litter and grit to which limestone chips have been added. The soil should be kept moist throughout the growing season. It flowers in June, July and early August.

GOODYERA

Goodyera is one of the larger terrestrial genera and one of the most widespread, well represented in both the Old and New Worlds and in both temperate and tropical climates. Many of the species are noted for their attractive foliage, which can be veined with white, silver or even gold, rather than for their relatively small and often drab flowers. The majority of species are tropical and subtropical and need not concern us here. A few species are worthy of cultivation, and these can be among the easier species to grow.

G.foliosa (Lindley)Bentham

G.foliosa is one of the largest of the temperate species both in habit and flower size, although it cannot match the 4–5 cm-long long flowers of *G.macrantha* Max. It has well-spaced pleated dark green leaves on a stout stem that can reach 30 cm or more tall from a fleshy creeping rhizome. The flowers are pink with white petals and a white lip borne in a dense spike but each overtopped by a long lanceolate bract.

This unusual orchid is native to China, Korea, Japan and the Ryukyu Islands where it grows in shaded places in woodland and forest. It grows well in a container in a protected place in a compost of leaf litter, loam and gritty sand (compost D, p.27), the rhizomes creeping through the top layer of the mix.

G.oblongifolia Raf.

The attractive dark green leaves marked with silvery veins and a broader silver mid-vein are the main feature of this North American species. It is

closely allied to the native British Creeping Lady's Tresses, *G.repens*, but is a much larger plant, up to 45 cm tall, with larger flowers, more than 5 mm long, borne in a lax elongated spiralling inflorescence.

It grows in the wild in both deciduous and coniferous forests in deep leaf litter and shade. In cultivation it should be grown in a compost rich in leafmould and chopped leaves, with a plentiful supply of grit and should be placed in a shaded spot. It will also do well in containers in compost D (see p.27).

G.repens (L.) R.Br
(FIGURE 32C)

The Creeping Lady's Tresses is a native British species mostly found in northern coniferous woods and in plantations in East Anglia. On the Continent, it is found in similar situation in northern Europe and in the mountains of central Europe. It is also widespread through Asia to Japan and in North America where it and related species are called Rattlesnake Plantains.

It is a creeping plant with almost prostrate leaves on a short stem arising from a creeping rhizome. The evergreen leaves are attractively veined with silver or pale green. The inflorescences, 8–25 cm long and produced from June until August, bear up to 20 small whitish glandular-hairy flowers arranged in an open spiral.

The closely related North American species, *G.pubescens* (Figure 32B, p.97), differs in its more heavily silver-netted leaves and the denser inflorescence of slightly larger white flowers.

Both of these species can be grown in shaded positions in the garden in a compost of peat, leafmould, gritty sand and added pine, fir or larch needles, or compost D (see p.27) in pots.

G.schlechtendaliana Reichb.f.
(FIGURE 32A)

Another species with attractively silver-veined leaves on a short stalk from which a slender inflorescence, 7.5–20 cm tall, arises. The flowers are pale pink, about 1 cm across, and open more widely than in other species.

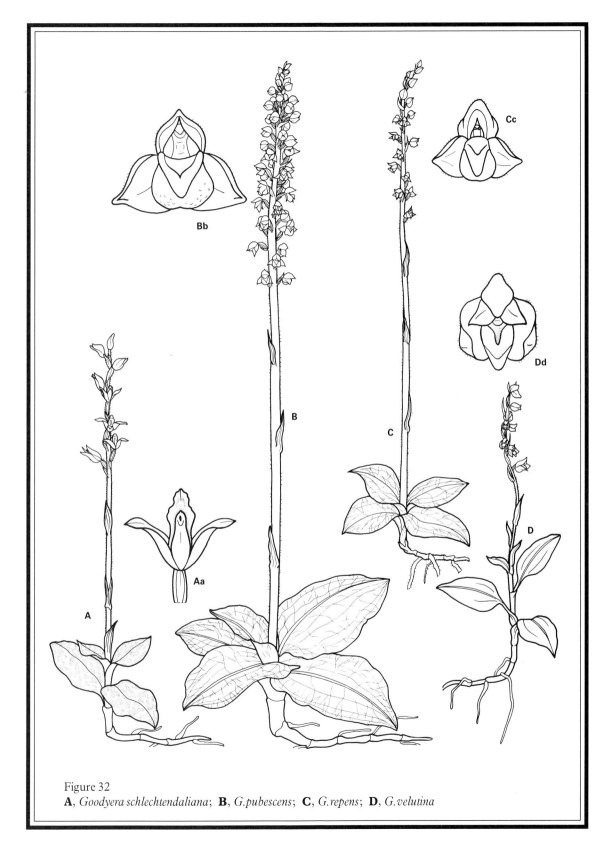

Figure 32
A, *Goodyera schlechtendaliana*; **B**, *G.pubescens*; **C**, *G.repens*; **D**, *G.velutina*

It is a native of Japan, China and Taiwan where it grows in stony places in pine and other forests. In cultivation it should be placed in a well-drained half shaded position in a compost of loam, decaying pine needles and gritty sand.

G.velutina Max.

(FIGURE 32D)

Another Eastern Asiatic species with strikingly marked leaves, 2–6.5 cm long, which are deep purple below and velvety dark green above with a central silver stripe on the mid-vein. The flowers are also among the prettiest in the genus with rose-pink flushed sepals, white petals and a white lip. The creeping rhizome is also usually purple while the floral axis is green or purple.

It grows in woodland and in forest from 600 to 2,000 m (1,965–6,560 ft) altitude in its native habitat. In cultivation, it should be placed in a sheltered, shaded position in a well-drained compost of loam, leafmould, pine needles and gritty sand. Greenhouse cultivation in compost D (see p.27) will also suit this species well.

GYMNADENIA

Only two species of *Gymnadenia* are known, and one of these, the Fragrant Orchid, *G.conopsea*, is a native species in the British Isles, one of the delights of a sunny day in late June on the chalk downs and other limestone grasslands in the country. The other species, *G.odoratissima*, is a smaller plant which is sometimes called the Short-spurred Fragrant Orchid. It grows in the mountains and also in calcareous marshes of central and southern Europe. Interestingly, it has been found once in northern England in the last century on the oolitic limestone in Durham.

G.conopsea (L.)R.Br.

(FIGURE 13C)

The Fragrant Orchid is one of the most elegant of the native British species. It can grow to 45 cm tall with a dense elongate spike, 6 to 16 cm long, with as many as 200 flowers in each head. The pinkish-purple flowers, although small and only a few mm

across, are as the vernacular name suggests, sweetly fragrant. White-flowered plants are sometimes found in the wild. The flowers have a three-lobed lip that lacks a callus but has a long slender spur, 11 to 18 mm long, at the base. The flowers are pollinated by butterflies. It is occasionally confused with the Pyramidal Orchid but that has a pyramidal-shaped inflorescence, and flowers with a callus on the lip.

G.conopsea is very widely distributed across Europe and Asia to Japan. Var.*densiflora* is a particularly robust orchid up to 80 cm tall, found growing in marshy areas throughout the range of the species. Its flowers have a noticeable scent of cloves.

This species will grow in a calcareous compost in full sun.

HIMANTOGLOSSUM

The Lizard Orchids are amongst the largest of the European and Middle Eastern orchids. They are very closely allied to *Orchis* and a number of other monotypic genera such as *Comperia* and *Barlia*, and are most easily distinguished by their elongate lip with a streamer-like mid-lobe. There are four or six species depending upon which authority is followed.

H.hircinum (L.)Sprengel

(FIGURE 21B)

This is a splendid plant that can reach 80 or 90 cm tall, with a stout stem with 6 to 8 lanceolate unspotted leaves at the base. The inflorescence carries 40 to 80 flowers, distinguished by their goaty smell, in a relatively dense head. The flowers have a small hood and a very long three-lobed lip, 3 to 5 cm long and shortly spurred at the base. The side lobes are short and incurved but the mid-lobe elongate, slender and bifid towards the apex.

The Lizard Orchid is one of the rarest native British orchids, found only in a few sites in the southern and eastern counties. Fortunately it is commoner elsewhere and can be seen in quantity on roadsides in south-western France before the mowers decapitate it. It grows in calcareous grassland but is best grown in a pot in compost C (see p. 27) with added limestone.

LIPARIS

Liparis is a cosmopolitan genus, most of whose species are tropical or subtropical. A few species are found in the temperate regions of the northern hemisphere with a single species, the Fen Orchid, *L.loeselii* (Figure 33C, p. 100), a rare member of the British flora. Its rarity is almost entirely due to the loss of its habitat, which has been drained. It is not a particularly suitable subject for cultivation as it is a small insignificant plant with small yellowish-green flowers, but it will readily grow in live *Sphagnum* moss.

A few of the species from the Far East are relatively easy to grow and charming in a modest way.

L.krameri Franch.& Sav.

This is typical of many of the Asiatic species with two pleated leaves produced from a fleshy conical or ovoid pseudobulb. The inflorescence, 7.5 to 15 cm long, carries about ten flowers in a short lax spike. The flowers are green and sometimes flushed with maroon with a more or less purple- or maroon-veined entire lip with an apiculate apex.

L.krameri grows well in a sheltered shaded and damp position on a raised peat bed, or in a container in compost D (see p. 27) in an alpine house. In the wild it grows in open woodland in shaded places in its native Japan and Korea.

L.kumokiri Maekwa

Another Japanese species which is taller than the preceding species but has smaller green flowers. These have very narrow sepals and petals and a short subquadrate strongly reflexed lip.

It tends to grow in colonies in the wild and is quite hardy in cultivation, preferring a position in a raised peat bed with plenty of added leafmould. It has survived outside at Kew in a sheltered position for some years.

L.liliiflora (L.)Lindl.
(FIGURE 33A)

This is the prettiest of the North American species, a delicate, but scarcely showy plant. It is small, rarely more than 20 cm tall, producing two shiny elliptic leaves from a 2 cm-long ovoid pseudobulb. The inflorescence bears up to 25 flowers. The sepals and petals are slender, and the flower is dominated by its decurved obovate pale purple lip with darker veins. It is close to the Japanese species *L.makinoana* (Figure 33B, p. 100).

It is found in the north-eastern United States where it grows in woodland along streams and in gulleys, and also in secondary woodland. It will form large colonies in suitable habitats. This species was first cultivated in the British Isles as early as 1797, when a plant grown outside in a sheltered border flowered for the Marquis of Blandford at Bill-hill in Berkshire.

LISTERA

A small genus of Old World orchids with two widespread species only. The popular name "Twayblade" in the British Isles describes the plants well because they have two large opposite leaves held well above the substrate and horizontal to it. They are not generally species that are showy enough to warrant planting in a garden but the Common Twayblade, *L.ovata*, is not uncommon in hedgerows and shrubby areas in and on the edge of gardens in Europe.

L.ovata (L.)R.Br.
(FIGURE 37C)

A very distinctive species that grows from 30 to 60 cm tall. The large paired basal leaves are more obvious than the slender spike of small green or reddish brown-flushed flowers. The latter are small, a centimetre or so long with a pendent oblong, apically bilobed but spurless lip at the lower side.

It is probably the most widespread and commonest orchid in north and central Europe and its range extends to the Mediterranean and across into central Asia, growing in a wide variety

Figure 33
A, *Liparis liliiflora;* **B**, *L.makinoana;* **C**, *L.loeselii*

of habitats from woodland and scrub to grassland on both calcicolous, neutral and acidic soils. It flowers from May to August depending on the altitude and latitude.

The Lesser Twayblade, *L.cordata*, is a plant of coniferous forest, bogs and moorland and is seldom to be found in cultivation. It is very widespread in nature both in Eurasia and North America.

OPHRYS

The bee and spider orchids of the genus *Ophrys* are predominantly Mediterranean plants but four species of the 40 or so are native in the British Isles. Two, the Bee Orchid, *O.apifera*, and the Fly Orchid, *O.insectifera*, are locally common, but the Early and Late Spider Orchids, *O.sphegodes* and *O.holoserica*, are two of the rarest British species.

Several of the Continental species are spectacular plants. The Mirror of Venus Orchid, *O.vernixia* (Figure 34C, p.102; also known as *O.speculum*), and Bertoloni's Bee Orchid, *O.bertolonii* (Figure 34B, p.102), have a shiny blue mirror-like area on the lip. Several others are also worth growing. However, they have an unjustified reputation for being difficult to grow and, so far as we are aware, few gardeners have had much success with them out of doors. They certainly respond best to pot cultivation. The mycorrhizal association seems to be important throughout the life cycle of these orchids. Disturbance of the plants if they are lifted during the growing season seems to be enough to tip the balance in favour of parasitism by the mycorrhizal fungus. They are also intolerant of the damp cold conditions that are common out of doors in the British winter.

We recommend cultivation in pots in an alpine house. Compost C (see p.27) with added limestone chips suits most species. An account of their successful cultivation is given by Bailes *et al.* (1986) and (also by Bailes *et al.*) in the *Orchid Review* (1987). It should be remembered that *Ophrys* are protected by law in most countries and should, on no account, be dug up from the wild.

The fascinating pollination biology of *Ophrys* species is discussed on page 8.

The genus is something of a taxonomic nightmare, with some authorities recognising about 30 species while others accept more than 50. Many of the species are quite distinct, but three species, *O.holoserica*, *O.sphegodes* and *O.scolopax* are particularly problematic. These are either very variable species which are actively evolving, so that several rather distinctive forms or varieties are recognisable, or else these variants can be treated as distinct species. Our view is that recognising many species distinguished on very minor features of lip and petal form is not particularly useful or realistic. We are happy to admit that for *Ophrys* we are lumpers rather than splitters.

O.apifera Huds.
(FIGURE 34A)

The common Bee Orchid is one of our favourite plants and its appearance signals the start of summer in the British Isles. It is a small plant usually no more than 25 cm tall but we have seen plants 50 cm or more tall on the Continent. The flowering spike is produced as the rosette of silvery-green leaves wither. The spike carries 3 to 9 flowers or rarely more. These have pink sepals and petals and a lip that resembles the body of a small Bumble Bee. Strangely, despite its shape, the Bee Orchid is not pollinated by a bee but is, uniquely in the genus, self pollinated.

Bee Orchids often appear, apparently spontaneously, in lawns, tennis courts and other grassy areas in gardens. They will multiply rapidly if the plants are allowed to flower and set seed before the grass is cut. In one old tennis court where a single rosette was spotted eight years previously, 130 flowering spikes appeared in 1988.

They can also be grown in pots in a calcareous well-drained compost and in full sun. During the summer months the tubers can be left to dry off in the pots and should be repotted in the autumn (see the instructions on p.33).

O.holoserica (Burm.f.)Greuter
(FIGURE 34D)

Though a rare species and on the verge of extinction in England, the Late Spider Orchid is not uncommon on the Continent particularly in the

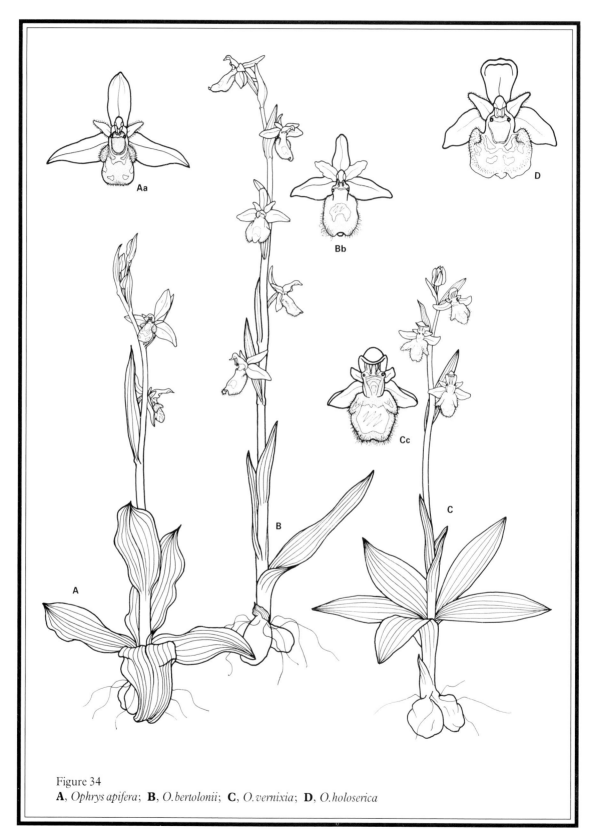

Figure 34
A, *Ophrys apifera*; **B**, *O. bertolonii*; **C**, *O. vernixia*; **D**, *O. holoserica*

Mediterranean region. It is a variable species characterised by pink sepals and petals and a brown hairy fan-shaped lip, with a complex yellow-margined speculum marking and a yellow protuberant apical attachment on the lip. Plants in northern Europe seldom attain 30 cm or have more than three or four flowers, but we have seen plants up to 80 cm tall with ten flowers in Turkey.

This species is another that grows through the winter and spring, flowering in May and early June in the wild. Specimens with the largest flowers are found in Crete and have been named as var. *grandiflora.*

This species is perhaps better known under the name *O.fuciflora* but that name has recently been shown to be a later synonym.

O.lutea Cav.

The Yellow Bee Orchid is probably the least insect-like species in the genus but nevertheless attractive for all that. It has pale green sepals and petals and a lip with a brown or bluish centre with a flat yellow margin. Specimens from the western Mediterranean, especially Spain, are the most attractive and have a broad bright yellow margin, while those from farther east generally have a narrower marginal band of yellow.

This species grows in open places in the maquis and garigue, often in full sun, in calcareous soils. It grows over the wet winter months, flowering in the spring as the basal rosette dies down.

O.tenthedrinifera Willd.

For some puzzling reason this splendid species has been given the ugly name of the Sawfly Orchid.

The three to eight flowers appear in April and May. The sepals and petals are pale pink, and the hairy lip has a small speculum inside a narrow brown area which is surrounded by a broad yellow zone. The sides of the lip are often strongly reflexed.

It is another Mediterranean species that is common in open places in scrub up to about 1,200 m (3,935 ft). It will survive well in cultivation if grown in a pot in an alpine house in compost C (see p.27) with added limestone chips.

ORCHIS

Some 37 species of *Orchis* are currently recognised as native to Europe and, of these, six are found in the British Isles. Two of these, the Military Orchid, *O.militaris,* and the Monkey Orchid, *O.simia,* are amongst the rarest of British plants and are considerably endangered in the wild. Fortunately both are commoner on the Continent. Sadly, the other native species are also declining throughout their ranges mainly because of the destruction of their habitats. The Green-winged Orchid, *O.morio,* is declining because it grows in wet meadows which are being agriculturally 'improved' by drainage and the addition of fertilisers and selective weedkillers. The orchids are the first plants to suffer from these activities.

The species of *Orchis* are as challenging to cultivate as the species of *Ophrys.* Again, it seems likely that the sensitive mycorrhizal relationship may preclude the easy transfer of plants into culture. However, when successfully transferred, *Orchis* plants may grow well for a few years but then disappear, suggesting that they may be short-lived perennials. It is important, therefore, to ensure that plants are propagated regularly to guard against this eventuality. In the garden, predation by slugs and snails will also rapidly deplete a stock unless preventive action is taken.

Of the native British species the most spectacular must be the Lady Orchid, *O.purpurea,* nowadays confined to a few woods in Kent. The Continental species *O.papilionacea,* the Butterfly Orchid of Linnaeus, and *O.italica,* the Italian Orchid, are also showy plants which can form large colonies in suitable habitats. These and the other Mediterranean species grow throughout the winter and spring months and would certainly need protection in Britain during that period. We would strongly recommend alpine house cultivation in compost C (see p.27) for most *Orchis* species.

O.coriophora L.

The Bug Orchid is one of the less showy species but is included here because it is easy to grow. The typical subspecies has a pyramidal head of small purple-spotted flowers with a marked three-lobed lip, and an unpleasant smell said to resemble that of bedbugs, hence the common name. It grows in damp grasslands usually on slightly acid soils throughout central Europe across to the Caucasus.

The commoner subsp. *fragrans*, however, has a sweetly scented and more attractive flower distinguished by its longer lip and longer spur. This subspecies is far commoner than the typical one and is widespread in the Mediterranean in grassland and garigue.

A closely allied and more attractive orchid is the Holy Orchid, *O. sancta*, a common species in Mediterranean Turkey and the Dodecanese. It has larger pale pink sweetly scented flowers, among the latest flowering of the Mediterranean species appearing in May and early June. It grows in sandy, calcareous soils in full sun. At Kew, *O. sancta* has responded well to cultivation in a frost-free glasshouse.

O.italica Poir.

The Italian Orchid is one of the choicest in the genus. It in many ways resembles *O. simia* but the flowers are slightly larger, with the lowest developing first, are pink and have more attenuate floral segments. Well-grown plants reach 40 cm tall and are robust with a conical head of up to 20 flowers.

It is a Mediterranean species that grows in calcareous soils in grassland, garigue and open places in pine woodland.

O.laxiflora Lam.
(FIGURE 35D)

This elegant orchid is almost a native species to Britain, just reaching the Channel Islands. It consequently is sometimes called the Jersey Orchid but the name Lax-flowered Orchid is probably preferable.

O. laxiflora can grow into a stately plant over a metre tall although 50-70 cm is perhaps more usual. The inflorescence is laxly 6- to 20-flowered and the flowers a rich deep purple with a white central streak and a few purple spots on the lip. It is widely distributed throughout central and south-

ern Europe and the Middle East, usually growing in wet grassland and marshes where it flowers between April and June.

It is one of the easier *Orchis* species in cultivation and should be grown in compost C (see p. 27).

O.mascula L.

The Early Purple Orchid is a native British species that has the distinction of an appearance in Shakespeare as 'long purples'. It is a variable species with several named subspecies throughout its range. The typical subspecies of western and central Europe is characterised by its spotted leaves and purple flowers, in which the lateral sepals lie reflexed and back to back and the lip is three-lobed with a prominent notched mid-lobe.

It is one of the commonest native British orchids, which often grows in association with Bluebells (*Scilla non-scriptus*) in deciduous woodland but is also found in hedgerows and in grassland. A hardy species, it is recorded up to 2,700 m (8,860 ft) in Continental Europe.

O.militaris L.
(FIGURE 35B)

This robust orchid is one of the rarest of British plants, but fortunately is locally common in parts of the Continent although, even there, it is declining. It grows from 30 to 65 cm tall and bears a dense conical head of many flowers. The sepals and petals form a greyish-pink hood over the four-lobed somewhat man-shaped lip, which is white and heavily spotted with purple tufts of hairs.

It is a plant of chalk and limestone grassland, and woodland margins and glades, up to 1,800 m (5,950 ft) elevation. In cultivation in the garden it requires an open calcareous compost in light shade. It will survive for many years, but rarely multiplies in cultivation.

O.morio L.
(FIGURE 35C)

The Green-winged Orchid is one of the commonest British orchids but sadly declining in most

Figure 35
A, *Orchis papilionacea*; **B**, *O.militaris*; **C**, *O.morio*; **D**, *O.laxiflora*

places because of habitat destruction and changes in land use. It is a species of wet grassland but is intolerant of fertilisers, herbicides and drainage activities.

This orchid is characterised by its hooded whitish or purplish sepals and petals, the lateral sepals bearing distinctive greenish veins. The lip is three-lobed with the sides reflexed and with an ascending clavate spur at the base, usually dark purple with a white central zone spotted with dark purple. Pale pink-flowered and albino forms are to be found in many localities.

The Green-winged Orchid occasionally appears in lawns where it will spread rapidly if allowed to set seed each year. The areas where it grows should not be mown until late July or early August. A fine colony of this attractive orchid thrives on the lawns of a convent in mid Sussex. Some of its best remaining habitats in southern England are in cemeteries.

The western Mediterranean species *O.longicornu* is closely allied to *O.morio*, but is more strikingly coloured with deep mauve side lobes to the lip and a longer ascending spur.

O.papilionacea L.

(FIGURE 35A)

The continental Pink Butterfly Orchid is a beautiful plant, 15 to 40 cm in height. It has a few-flowered conical head of large showy flowers. The sepals and petals are tapering and form a prominent dull dark purple hood over the large entire fan-shaped lip. The lip is white or pink speckled or flushed with darker pink and has a short spur at its base. The species is variable in both flower size and coloration and several of the geographical variants have received taxonomic recognition.

O.papilionacea is a Mediterranean species found in dry grassland, garigue, maquis and open woodland on calcareous soils in full sun. It flowers over a long season, from January until early May.

OREORCHIS

Oreorchis is a small genus of about 12 species from northern India, China, Korea and Japan. At first sight it most closely resembles a *Calanthe*, *Crem-* *astra* or *Spathoglottis* in habit but the flowers are smaller and quite distinct.

O.patens Lindl.

(FIGURE 36A)

Two apical pleated lanceolate leaves emerge from the most recent of an underground string of onion-like pseudobulbs. The inflorescence is lateral and can range from 30 to 45 cm tall with a lax terminal spike of about 20 flowers. The sepals and petals are yellow and the three-lobed lip whitish. The lip has ligulate forward-pointing side lobes and a two-ridged callus, but lacks a spur.

The pseudobulbs should be shallowly buried in an open compost of peat, loam and leaf litter and can be grown in a sheltered partly shaded position on a rock garden or raised bed in the milder parts of the British Isles, or in an alpine house elsewhere. In the wild, it grows in woods up to 3,500 m (11,480 ft) elevation.

PLATANTHERA

The genus *Platanthera* is closely related to *Habenaria*, probably the largest genus of terrestrial orchids, and is included therein by some authors. However, in both Europe and North America, *Platanthera* is kept distinct in recent publications and we shall follow that treatment here.

Platantheras are characterised by fleshy roots, mostly without tubers, a dorsal sepal and entire petals that form a hood over the column, recurved lateral sepals and an unlobed lip that may have a lacerate margin. The stigma lobes are sessile whereas in *Habenaria* they are usually stalked. They are usually pollinated by butterflies or moths attracted to the nectariferous spur at the base of the lip. When contact is made with the column the pollen masses are removed on the insect's head or eyes.

The American species with fringed lips have been placed in the genus *Blephariglottis* by some authors but most recent accounts do not maintain this as distinct from *Platanthera*.

Case (1987) recommends growing the North American species in a sand-peat bed or in pots in pure living *Sphagnum* moss where they will thrive.

Figure 36
A, *Oreorchis patens*; **B**, *Pogonia japonica*; **C**, *Ponerorchis graminifolia*

His sand-peat compost is a mixture of 60 per cent silica sand and 40 per cent *Sphagnum* peat. The bed, preferably raised, should be mulched with coarse pine needles (*Pinus sylvestris*).

P.blephariglottis (Willd.)Lindley

This orchid, known in the United States as the Large White Fringed Orchid, is very closely allied to *P.ciliaris* being distinguished mainly on flower colour. It is a robust species 30 cm to almost a metre tall in suitable sites. It has 2 to 4 glossy green leaves and an inflorescence of 30 to 50 flowers in a loose to dense cylindrical head. The flowers are pure white and are characterised by the spathulate lip which is longly fringed on the margins of the apical two-thirds.

It is a common orchid in the eastern seaboard states of North America, from Texas to Maryland, growing in wet places such as bogs. It flowers several weeks earlier than *P.ciliaris* except in Florida where the latter flowers first.

P.chlorantha Custer ex Reichb.f.
(FIGURE 37B)

The Greater Butterfly Orchid is one of the two native British species, the other being the Lesser Butterfly Orchid, *P.bifolio* (Figure 37A, p.109). They both have two basal elliptic glossy leaves and lax inflorescences of several fragrant, white or greenish-white flowers with an entire ligulate lip and slender elongate spur. *P.chlorantha* is distinguished by its widely spaced divergent anther loculi which in *P.bifolia* are parallel and close together. Hybrids are not uncommon in the wild.

Both species are widely scattered throughout Europe and east to the Caucasus. *P.chlorantha* grows in deciduous woodland often in deep shade and on the edges of woods and thickets usually on calcareous soils. It flowers between mid-June and August, usually but not always before *P.bifolia*. That species is more tolerant in its habitat preference and will also grow in open moorland and on heaths. Both species will grow well in the garden, or in containers in compost C (see p.27).

In North Africa and the Middle East, forms with green flowers but otherwise scarcely distinguishable from the European species have been named as *P.algeriensis* and *P.holmboei* respectively.

P.dilatata, a North American species that resembles a large *P.bifolia*, has grown well in the woodland garden conditions at Kew for a number of years.

P. ciliaris (L.)Lindley

The Yellow Fringed Orchid is one of the prettiest terrestrial orchids in North America. It is a large plant growing to 1 metre tall in favourable localities. Two to four glossy lanceolate leaves, 5 to 20 cm long, are borne on the lower part of the stem. The inflorescence comprises 30 to 60 yellow or orangy-yellow flowers in a lax to dense cylindrical head. The distinctive feature of the flowers is the lip which is entire but has a deeply fringed margin.

It is widespread in eastern North America from Texas and Florida as far north as upstate New York. It grows in bogs, fields and woods in both wet and well-drained soils and in full sun or partial shade, flowering from late June to late September depending on the latitude. This species was first flowered in the British Isles in 1797 by J. Lyons, gardener to the Marquis of Blandford, who grew it in a shady border in a mixture of loam and peat.

P.grandiflora (Bigelow)Lindley

The Large Purple Fringed Orchid is a handsome plant growing up to 120 cm tall, with 2 to 6 green lanceolate cauline leaves and a head of 30 to 60 large purple flowers. These are distinguished by their flat three-lobed lip which has an emarginate mid-lobe that gives it almost a four-lobed appearance. Each lobe is deeply fringed. The base of the lip at the mouth of the 2.5 cm-long slender spur is white.

It is distributed from the Great Lakes across to the eastern seaboard of the United States and north to Newfoundland. It flowers some two weeks before the smaller but similar *P.psycodes*.

Figure 37
A, *Platanthera bifolia*; **B**, *P.chlorantha*; **C**, *Listera ovata*

P.psycodes (L.)Lindley

This species is closely allied to the rarer *P.grandiflora* and can easily be mistaken for it. It differs in being a smaller plant, up to 90 cm tall, and by its flowers where the fringe lacerations are less than one-third the depth of the lip, the smaller and relatively narrow column with scarcely divergent anther loculi, and the dumbbell shape of the mouth of the spur.

It grows luxuriantly and commonly in roadside ditches, damp meadows, on the edges of bogs, in damp open woods and in the rocky beds of mountain streams in the north-east of North America from the Great Lakes to Newfoundland.

PLEIONE

Pleione is a small genus of about 16 species closely related to the predominently tropical genus *Coelogyne*. It differs, however, in having annual pseudobulbs and one-flowered inflorescences of pink, purple or, less commonly, yellow or white flowers. The distribution of *Pleione* ranges from Nepal and northern India across to China and Taiwan. The genus has undergone a revival in popularity over the past ten years or so, mainly due to the large number of new hybrids that have been bred to increase both the range of flower colour and shape available, and extend the flowering season from late September to early June.

They are popularly called 'Windowsill orchids' or 'Nepalese crocuses' and are not generally considered to be hardy plants, being thought to need protection from the combination of damp and frosty winter weather prevalent in the British Isles. However, some of the species and hybrids will survive and even thrive outside in a sheltered spot in the garden and have proved hardy even in severe winter weather. A patch of *Pleione limprichtii* grown outside in Suffolk survived 17° of frost (15°F) in the winter of 1986 while several growers have had similar success with a range of other cultivars and species.

The successful cultivation of pleiones out of doors depends upon selection of a suitable spot and providing a suitable sharply drained open compost. It is perhaps not surprising that some

species are hardy in Britain. *P.bulbocodioides* and *P.limprichtii* grow in the high mountains of south-western China up to 3,600 m (11,810 ft) elevation, while the rare *P.scopulorum* has been recorded from over 4,000 m (13,125 ft) on the Burmese-Chinese border. The best-known species and most widely available in the nursery trade is *P.formosana* from Taiwan, another montane plant, which is hardy in outside frames if kept dry over the winter. It is also the parent of many of the finer hybrids and transmits its hardiness to them.

A detailed account of the genus, its classification and its cultivation are given in Cribb & Butterfield (1988). A compost based on pine bark chips (compost A, p.26), or the loam-based compost D (see p.27) is suitable for all pleiones.

P.bulbocodioides (Franch.)Rolfe

For many years this species was represented in cultivation in the British Isles by a single but vigorous clone which was mistakenly named as *P.yunnanensis* (Figure 38B, p.112), which is a distinct sympatric species. Many new introductions have, however, recently been made and are now widely available in trade.

It is a spring-flowering species with a pink or, more commonly, rose-purple solitary flower borne on an erect 6–20 cm-long stalk which emerges from the base of an ovoid, green or dull purple pseudobulb. The solitary pleated erect lanceolate leaf appears from the new shoot after the flower has opened. The spreading and falcate sepals and petals are concolorous, while the trumpet-shaped lip is spotted with red-purple and has four or five irregular lamellate callus ridges along its central veins.

In the wild, *P.bulbocodioides* grows on rocky slopes in open pine forests under *Rhododendron* and other ericaceous shrubs. The pseudobulbs grow in a leaf litter of pine needles and leafmould buried 2 or 3 cm below the surface. In cultivation the pseudobulbs are often grown on the surface of the compost but out of doors they should always be buried to provide some protection against frosts.

P.formosana Hay.

(FIGURE 38C)

P.formosana is the largest-flowered of the spring-flowering species. It can produce a large rather flattened pseudobulb, 3–4 cm across, and a well-grown one can produce two or even three flowering shoots. The flowers, produced on an erect 6–12 cm-tall stalk, have pink to rose-purple sepals and petals and a white or whitish lip marked with yellow, orange or red spots. The single pleated leaf develops with the inflorescence and matures long after the flower drops. White-flowered forms with a yellow-spotted lip are not uncommon in cultivation, the best being the cultivar 'Clare'.

P.formosana is native to Taiwan from where thousands of pseudobulbs are exported every year. It grows there in the mountains in open forests in deep leaf litter, forming large colonies if left undisturbed. It can be grown either in pot-culture where it may be repotted every second year, or it may be tried outside where it needs some protection against the base of a tree or under a shrub. It will survive quite happily in a typical *Pleione* compost or even on a peat block, providing the pseudobulbs are buried below the surface.

One of the finest hybrids of *P.formosana*, with *P.limprichtii*, is *P.*Versailles of which 'Bucklebury' (which has a First Class Certificate from the Royal Horticultural Society) is an outstanding and vigorous clone suited to the garden. *P.*Alishan, *P.formosana* × *P.*Versailles, is another worth considering for its attractive flowers, with pink sepals and petals tipped with white and a white lip, boldly spotted with reddish-purple, held on an erect spike well above the substrate. *P.*Tolima, *P.formosana* × *P.speciosa*, is one of the most vividly coloured hybrids and another that is hardy. It will often produce two flowers on each flower stalk and these are dark rose-purple with a heavily red-spotted lip with bright yellow or white callus ridges.

P.forrestii Schltr.

The sensational *P.forrestii* has revolutionised *Pleione* breeding, introducing its yellow flower colour into a range of hybrids. The flowers are produced in the spring on a short stalk, 4–8 cm long, from a large conical green pseudobulb. The flower colour can vary from pale primrose to deep buttercup-yellow with a red-spotted lip. Albino forms are also reported in the wild.

This splendid orchid is native to western Yunnan where it grows on the wetter slopes of the mountains at up to 2,900 m (9,515 ft). It is probably not quite hardy in the British Isles and should be grown in a pot in a frost-free glasshouse for the best results.

The plant grown for so many years as *P.forrestii* has been conclusively shown to be a hybrid of that species with the rare *P.albiflora*. This hybrid is now called *P.* × *confusa*. It is one parent of *P.*Shantung, the most spectacular and vigorous of all *Pleione* hybrids. We have seen plants of this with 5 cm pseudobulbs, a 30 cm-long leaf and two or three inflorescences each bearing two or three flowers. These vary from very pale pink to primrose-yellow, spotted with red on the lip.

P.limprichtii Schltr.

Dr Harry Smith, the Swedish collector and botanist, introduced *P.limprichtii* into cultivation from the mountains of western Sichuan in China. He sent plants to Magnus Johnson (1986) who has written a graphic account of its discovery and cultivation in the *Kew Magazine*.

P.limprichtii has small ovoid pseudobulbs which produce a single-flowered inflorescence in the spring. The flowers are rose-purple with a red-spotted lip almost circular in outline. The solitary leaf develops after the flower has appeared. This species is closely related to *P.bulbocodioides* and the spectacular rose-purple-flowered *P.speciosa* but differs in its lip shape and callus structure.

It is the hardiest of the readily available species. In China, it is found at 3,000–3,600 m (9,840–11,810 ft), growing in a thin humus-rich soil, often only 2.5 cm thick, on moss-covered limestone boulders in exposed situations. In the spring, the melt water from the snow on the hills above drains through the soil. In the wild, it produces colonies and will behave similarly in cultivation if left undisturbed for a few years.

P.limprichtii grows well in pans like other

Figure 38
A, *Pleione praecox*; **B**, *P. yunnanensis*; **C**, *P. formosana*

species but, if tried outside, should be placed in a sheltered place under shrubs or at the foot of a tree and in a gritty peaty fibrous compost. It will even grow well buried in a peat block. A covering of loose twigs and leaves will protect the pseudobulbs from severe frosts but in wet places it is also advisable to cover the plants with a tile or a sheet of glass.

P.praecox (J.E.Sm.)D.Don
(FIGURE 38A)

This Himalayan species is the hardiest of the autumn-flowering pleiones but will need protection from frost in most places. It is readily recognised when not in flower by its two-leaved pseudobulbs which are shortly cylindrical and flask-shaped with distinctive red and green markings and the bracts which are pustular. The flowers are amongst the largest in the genus with pink to rose-coloured sepals and petals and a pink-edged lip with yellow papillate callus ridges. A beautiful white-flowered variant called 'Everest' is in cultivation.

In the wild *P.praecox* grows as a terrestrial or lithophyte on steep mossy banks from 1200–3400 m altitude where it often forms sizeable colonies.

POGONIA

This small genus has representatives in both Asia and North America. Of these, *P.japonica* and *P.ophioglossoides* are the only species likely to be seen in cultivation.

P.japonica Reichb.f.
(FIGURE 36B)

P.japonica is a slender inconspicuous plant when not in flower, with a single ligulate leaf borne in the middle of an erect stem about 10–25 cm tall. The suberect flower is terminal and surprisingly large for such a delicate plant. It is about 2 cm long with white or pink segments and a lip with a darker purple margin and a white bearded callus.

In the wild, in Japan, it grows in damp places in open unshaded spots at altitudes up to 2,500 m

(8,200 ft). To appreciate its full beauty it should be grown in a pot (using compost D, p. 27), or in a raised position in a peat bed or rock garden in a suitable damp but well-drained compost. The margins of a stream would also be suitable if competition from other plants is avoided.

P.ophioglossoides (L.)Jussieu

This is very closely allied to the previous species but is usually a taller plant with a broadly elliptic leaf. It has a remarkably wide distribution from North America to China and Korea. *P.ophioglossoides* grows in colonies in the wild in open situations in *Sphagnum* bogs, marshes and on lake margins. It should be grown in a deep peaty compost or in *Sphagnum* in cultivation.

PONERORCHIS

A small genus allied to *Gymnadenia* and *Orchis* from China and Japan. All are dwarf plants with a few slender grass-like leaves on a slender stem which grows from an ovoid or ellipsoidal fleshy tuber. Both species mentioned here will grow well in a woodland compost D (see p. 27) in pots, in a shady spot in an alpine house.

P.graminifolia Reichb.f.
(FIGURE 36C)

This orchid reaches 10–15 cm, tall with the grass-like foliage setting off the few delicate pink flowers borne in an almost conical head at the apex of the stem. The flowers are relatively large for the size of the plant, over 1 cm across and with a 2 cm-long slightly decurved spur at the base of the prominently three-lobed lip. The flower looks very much like that of *Dactylorhiza fuchsii* in general appearance.

P.graminifolia is best grown in a pot or in an elevated place in a raised bed. It prefers a damp spot in a peaty compost.

P.chusua (D.Don)Soó

This Himalayan orchid is an attractive species with 10 to 25 cm tall stems, linear leaves up to

7.5 cm long and a few bright purple flowers. The flowers have reflexed lateral sepals and a three-lobed lip with equal lobes and an appressed short spur.

In nature it grows in open places and under shrubs on steep slopes from 2,400–4,200 m (7,875–13,780 ft) elevation.

PTEROSTYLIS

A genus of about 80 species, all but two from Australia and New Zealand, these orchids are popularly called 'greenhoods' because of their distinctive flowers. Only those species from the southern margins of Australia, southern New Zealand and Tasmania are likely to be at all hardy. The species grow through the British winter and spring and this makes them unlikely to be hardy, except in the mildest parts of the South-west.

The species can be conveniently divided into colony- and non-colony-forming types, the former being easier in cultivation. Many of these are easily grown in pots kept in a frost-free glass-house, and several will multiply rapidly and flower freely in such conditions.

The increasing popularity of growing native orchids in Australia has led to the appearance of several species in the nursery trade in the British Isles over the last year or two. We anticipate that they will feature increasingly in catalogues in the future, particularly as many have been success-fully grown from seed and propagated in large quantities.

Pterostylis are best planted as dormant tubers at a depth of about 3 cm in compost E (see p. 27), the Australian terrestrial mix. As with most Australian species, it should be remembered that *Pterostylis* will not tolerate calcareous soils. Plants should be lightly shaded, and will do best with a minimum night temperature of 4–5°C (39–41°F). All are autumn and winter growers.

A detailed account of the successful culture of Australian terrestrial orchids is provided by Richards (1985) in the *Orchid Review*.

P.alata (Labill.)Reichb.f.
(FIGURE 39A)

This delicate orchid produces rosettes of leaves on sterile shoots and separate fertile shoots that are leafy along the stem. The fertile shoots reach 10 to 25 cm tall with about four radical bract-like leaves and are one-, or rarely two-flowered at the apex. The flowers are 2 to 3 cm long with an acute forwards pointing whitish hood boldly veined with green at the base and dark brown above. The lateral sepals are united in their basal third and have two attenuate erect dark brown tails rising well above the hood.

It is a common species in south-eastern Australia and Tasmania, growing in sandy scrub-lands near the coast and inland in dry sclerophyl-lous forest.

P.baptistii R.D.Fitzgerald

P.baptistii's common name, the King Greenhood, is appropriate as it is one of the largest species in the genus. It has a basal rosette of 5 to 7 cm-long elliptic or lanceolate stalked leaves. The inflores-cence is single-flowered and can reach 35 cm tall. The flower is large, translucent and up to 5 cm long. Its hood is strongly concave, whitish and veined with green in the basal part and reddish-brown above. The lateral sepals have long attenu-ate erect apices rising above the hood.

P.baptistii prefers shaded places in dense scrub usually near streams or swamps where it can form extensive colonies. It is one of the commonest in cultivation in Britain.

P.coccinea R.D.Fitzgerald
(FIGURE 39E)

P.coccinea is a slender species 12 to 22 cm tall with fertile shoots and sterile rosettes as well. Its name derives from its flower which is veined and flushed with rusty-red. The flower is large with a 5 to 7 cm-long hood with a drawn-out apex. The lateral sepals are fused in the basal third and have atennuate ascending tails that rise well above the hood.

It is endemic to eastern New South Wales

Figure 39
A, *Pterostylis alata*; **B**, *P.concinna*; **C**, *P.truncata*; **D**, *P.nutans*; **E**, *P.coccinea*

where it is found in open grassland on the tablelands.

P.concinna R.Br.

(FIGURE 39B)

This, a widespread species in Eastern Australia from Queensland to Victoria, is a delicate plant with a rosette of small leaves, 1 to 3 cm long at the base. The flowers are usually solitary at the apex of a slender 5 to 30 cm-long stem. The 1 to 2 cm-long hood of the flower curves strongly forwards and is usually whitish and marked with bold green veins and a reddish tip. The lateral sepals are united in the basal half and have slender drawn-out erect red-brown tips.

It grows in sandy places in coastal scrub, often forming large colonies in the wild.

P.cucullata R.Br.

This is one of the larger flowered colony-forming greenhoods with flowering stems 5 to 30 cm long. The leaves are large, up to 10 cm long, ovate-oblong to elliptic in shape and usually crowded together. The flower is about 3 cm long and is brown or green with brown petals and lateral sepals. The bract subtending the flower is large and envelops the ovary and base of the flower.

It grows in sandy coastal heathland in Victoria and South Australia but in Tasmania extends its range into the mountains. It is a winter- and early spring-flowering species.

P.curta R.Br.

P.curta is one of the freest growing of all species in cultivation and has appeared with increasing frequency in Britain in recent years. It is a robust plant with a basal rosette of leaves that often have crisped margins. The inflorescence is one-flowered and from 10 to 30 cm tall. The 2 to 3.5 cm-long sturdy flower, held suberect at the apex, has an erect whitish concave hood, veined with green and with a red-brown apex. The lateral sepals are fused to beyond the middle and have short tapering tips that do not overtop the flower.

It is a widespread species from south-eastern

Queensland to South Australia and also New Caledonia, growing in temperate woodland in cool moist shaded gulleys where it can form large colonies.

P.fischii W.H. Nicholls

The 15 to 20 cm long fertile shoots of *P.fischii* have only very few cauline bract-like leaves along their length. The flower is white with green veins below and red-brown ones above. It has a hood about 2.5 cm long with a long drawn-out pendent tip. The lateral sepals are united in the basal quarter and have long drawn-out tapering erect tips that rise well above the flower.

It is found in the mountains of eastern New South Wales, but in coastal situations in Victoria, growing in light forest in sandy poor soils.

P.nutans R.Br.

(FIGURE 39D)

The common name of this distinctive orchid is the Nodding or Parrot's-beak Orchid. It is one of the greenest of the greenhoods, having a basal rosette of about five leaves with undulate or crispate margins. The single nodding flower is usually borne at the apex of a 10 to 30 cm-tall stalk. The hood of dorsal sepal and petals which is deeply concave and 1.5 to 3 cm long, is green with reddish-brown tips. The lateral sepals are joined in their basal half but divided above into short ascending tails about 1 cm long.

It is a common orchid throughout eastern temperate Australia where it grows in sheltered places in light forest undergrowth, especially in sandy areas by the coast. In the wild it flowers from July to October, the Australian late winter and spring.

P.obtusa R.Br.

Another delicate species with fertile and sterile shoots. The sterile shoots have a rosette of undulate margined leaves. The radical leaves on the fertile shoots are ovate and acute. The solitary flower, whitish with green veins and a brownish apex, is 1.8 to 3 cm long. The hood has a shortly

116

attenuate apex and the lateral sepals are fused in the basal third and drawn out into erect subclavate tips that rise above the hood.

It is a widespread species found in a variety of habitats in eastern Australia but most frequently on rocky wooded slopes in the hills and along the banks of streams. It can be locally common thereabouts.

P.truncata R.D.Fitzgerald
(FIGURE 39C)

The Brittle Greenhood, so named because the hood breaks easily, is another with both sterile and fertile growths, the former being a rosette of leaves while the latter bear leaves along the stem and have a large terminal flower. It is a dwarf species with the fertile stems 5 to 10 cm tall. The flower is very large for the size of the plant with a suberect deeply concave hood 3.5 to 5 cm long. The hood is whitish and longitudinally striped with dark green and reddish-brown. The lateral sepals are fused almost to half-way and finish in long slender ascending tails rising above the hood.

It is a local orchid in New South Wales and Victoria growing in grassland and heathland where it can form sizeable colonies.

SATYRIUM

This is a predominantly African genus of about 100 species, with a few species being found in Madagascar and Asia. Only a few Asiatic species are hardy or nearly so. The genus is allied to *Disa* but is readily distinguished by its globose or hooded dorsal sepal which has two spurs emerging from the back.

S.nepalense D.Don

A stately ground orchid, *S.nepalense* stands 50–75 cm tall from a basal rosette of leaves. The flowers are a bright pink, 10–13 cm across, borne in a dense spike 2.5–15 cm long.

It is a widespread and common orchid from Pakistan across to south-west China, at altitudes from 1,500–4,000 m (4,920–13,125 ft), growing in grassland and open scrub and flowering between July and September. A large container and woodland compost D (see p.27) suits this species well, with alpine house protection.

S.ciliatum Lindl. from Nepal and Tibet is similar in habit and flower colour but is distinguished by its ciliate petals and sepals.

SERAPIAS

The six known species of Tongue Orchid are essentially Mediterranean plants distributed eastwards to Turkey. A single species, *S.cordigera*, reaches Brittany in France but never succeeded in crossing the Channel.

Most of the species can be grown easily in compost C (see p.27) in pots or a raised bed or frame, or in a well-protected spot in the garden. They will form sizeable colonies if allowed.

S.cordigera L.

The Heart-lipped Tongue Orchid is widespread in western and southern Europe as far east as Greece and the Greek Islands. It can grow from 20–35 cm tall and bears a few relatively large flowers in April and May. The flowers have a hood of pale purple sepals and petals, lined with darker veins, and a heart-shaped pendent deep maroon lip which can reach 2.5 cm long.

It is a common sight on roadside verges in the Mediterranean region, forming large colonies in places, and is one of few plants that can survive the suffocating carpet of the Hottentot Figs, *Carpobrotus edulis* and *C.acinaciforme*, which have invaded so much of the region.

S.lingua L.
(FIGURE 40A)

Plants of the delicate *S.lingua* stand 10 to 30 cm tall with 4 to 5 linear-lanceolate leaves. The new tubers are borne on short stolons allowing colonies to develop rapidly. The flowers have greenish- to reddish-purple sepals and petals in a hood over the rather short ovate lip. The lip can be variable in colour from yellow to purple with both colour forms often occurring in the same colony.

This species is the easiest to distinguish in the

Figure 40
A, *Serapias lingua*; **B**, *S. vomeracea*; **C**, *S. neglecta*

genus and is characterised by the single raised callus at the base of the lip.

It is widespread in the Mediterranean region growing in damp meadows, olive groves, marshes and dune slacks, where it flowers in April and May.

S. neglecta De Not.
(FIGURE 40C)

This is the rarest species in the genus and also the largest-flowered. It reaches from 10 to 30 cm tall and bears 3 to 8 flowers in a dense inflorescence. The helmet of sepals and petals varies from light yellowish-green to deep purple. The ovate lip is large and broad, with two raised basal calli and varies from yellow to maroon in colour.

S.neglecta is found in scattered localities in southern France, Italy, Corsica, Sardinia and Yugoslavia, where it grows in olive groves, maquis, light woodland and damp meadows. It flowers from March until early May.

S.vomeracea (Burm.f.)Briq.
(FIGURE 40B)

The tallest-growing of the tongue orchids, *S.vomeracea* will grow up to 50 cm tall. Four to ten flowers are borne in a robust but lax spike. The long bracts overtopping the flowers are a useful distinguishing feature of this species. Its flowers have a pale purple or red hood of sepals and petals with darker veins and a long lanceolate lip, 9–11 cm long, ranging from pale to deep purple or red.

This species is widespread in the Mediterranean region as far east as Turkey and as far north as southern Switzerland. It grows in a variety of habitats from roadsides and grassy meadows to maquis and pine woods.

SPIRANTHES

Spiranthes are called Lady's Tresses Orchids because of their tightly spiralling inflorescences that are reminiscent of hair plaits. The genus is a large one with most of the species tropical or subtropical. However, three species are found in Europe, a few in temperate Asia and some 20 species in North America. The European species are all native in the British Isles but the Summer Lady's Tresses, *S.aestivalis*, is now sadly extinct. The Irish Lady's Tresses, *S.romanzoffiana*, found in a few places in Ireland, the West Country and western Scotland is one of the few European plants found also in North America. The third species, the Autumn Lady's Tresses, *S.spiralis*, is one of the commonest British orchids and the latest flowering of all, pushing up its flowering spikes in late August and September. Most species grow well in a woodland compost D (see p.27) in containers, and several are hardy enough to survive well in the open garden.

S.cernua (L.)L.C.Rich.

This is typical of the most of the North American species, a tall plant reaching 50 cm in height and with a tight spiral of pure white flowers in the apical third. It has 3 to 6 linear-oblanceolate basal leaves growing from a fascicle of swollen roots. The flowers are 9 to 11 mm long and the lip, which is recurved towards the apex, has a pale yellow mark in the centre.

In nature it grows on the wet margins of lakes and streams, in wet marshes and meadows and in wet woods. It is found as far north as Canada, and specimens from the northern part of its range are perfectly hardy in southern Britain. We have grown this species in both bog conditions and in normal composts.

S.lacera (Raf.)Raf.

This dwarf North American species is not unlike *S.spiralis* in general appearance, but it has a basal rosette of small leaves which persist when the orchid flowers and a longer stem up to 50 cm tall. The inflorescence carries 20 to 40 white flowers in an open spiral. The flowers are 4 to 5 mm long.

It is widespread in north central and north-eastern North America north to Nova Scotia growing in open woods and grassy meadows.

S.ochroleuca (Rybd.)Rydb.

This species is very close to *S.cernua*, differing in growing a little taller to 50 cm, in its yellowish flowers and the base of the lip which is not dilated but has large basal tuberosities.

It has a restricted distribution in the north-eastern United States and adjacent Canada as far north as Newfoundland. It grows in slightly drier places than *S.cernua* in meadows and woodland. Case (1987) suggests that it is readily cultivated.

S.romanzoffiana Chamisso

This species was originally described from a specimen collected in Alaska early in the last century, but it is widespread throughout northern America and has a few scattered outposts in the British Isles where it is known as the Irish Lady's Tresses.

In Britain it rarely reaches 25 cm in height but in North America can reach 50 cm in favourable places. It has 3 to 6 basal and cauline leaves and a tight spiral of up to 50 or so white flowers, 8 to 13 mm long.

It grows in a wide variety of habitats from bogs to open woodland and wet grassland. In North America it has also been found in the northern tundra, on the cliffs by the sea in California and by calcareous hot springs in Yellowstone National Park. At Kew, it has been grown out of doors for a number of years in a raised peat bed to which loam and leafmould have been added.

S. sinensis (Pers.)Ames

This pretty little orchid is widespread in Asia from the Himalayas across to Taiwan and south into the Pacific Islands and Australia. It is a delicate orchid with a spiral of tiny pink or white flowers, 4–5 mm long.

Some clones will grow well in a frost-free glasshouse in an open sandy mix with loam, leaf litter and a little added peat. It is one of the few orchids that grows easily from seed and seedlings are apt to pop up in pots all over the glasshouse.

S.spiralis (L.)Chevall.

A widespread orchid in Central and Southern Europe and the Middle East, the Autumn Lady's Tresses is often overlooked because it flowers so late in the year.

It is a dainty plant, 10–35 cm tall, that often forms colonies. The shortly but densely pubescent inflorescences arising from a basal rosette, and the small pubescent flowers, 6–7 mm long, are borne in a tight spiral. The flowers do not open widely and have white segments with a bright green mark on the lip.

A lucky few have *S.spiralis* in their lawns, especially where the gardens are on chalk or chalk turf has been used to create a lawn. Care must be taken so that the young inflorescences are not cut when the lawn is mown.

THELYMITRA

The Sun Orchids are one of the most attractive of the Australasian terrestrial genera. The genus comprises about 40 species, the majority in Australia and New Zealand but with a single species each in New Caledonia, New Guinea and Java.

It is a distinctive genus characterised by its flowers which are at first sight almost regular with the sepals, petals and lip similar. The column is, however, zygomorphic with lateral wings and two apical processes, which are usually adorned with tufts at the apex. Most of the species have mauve, blue or bluish flowers but white-, yellow- and red-flowered species are known. The most remarkable species is the Queen of Sheba Orchid, *T.variegata*, from Western Australia, which has flowers of iridescent red, purple and yellow. Thelymitras only open their flowers fully in sunshine and the British weather can frustrate even the most willing species.

They are best suited to pot culture in the alpine house in compost E (see p. 00), with a night minimum of about 4–5°C (39–41°F).

T.antennifera (Gunn ex Lindl.) Hook.f.

A slender plant up to 25 cm tall with a terete channelled basal leaf. The flowers, 2.5–3.5 cm across, are primrose yellow with a reddish flush on

Figure 41
A, *Thelymitra aristata*; **B**, *T.ixioides*

the outer surface of the sepals. The column has two deep maroon tufts at the apex.

This is a widespread species from southern New South Wales to South Australia and also in northern Tasmania and south western Australia growing in open forest and heathland and flowering from early spring until early summer. It has a tendency to be rather difficult to keep in cultivation for any length of time.

T.aristata Lindl.

(FIGURE 41A)

The Scented Sun Orchid is a variable species, 20 to 100 cm tall, with a basal rather flat lanceolate leaf up to 25 cm long. The inflorescence is usually few-flowered but well-grown specimens may have up to 35 flowers. These are 2 to 4.5 cm across, usually scented and range in colour from pink to purple or violet. The column is hooded and the apical projections are adorned with white hair tufts resembling small shaving brushes.

This attractive orchid is widespread in Australia and also in New Zealand, growing in a variety of habitats from open marshes in full sun to the shaded floors of primaeval forests. In more open situations it can form large colonies.

T.ixioides Sw.

(FIGURE 41B)

Like the preceding species, *T.ixioides* is a variable and widespread orchid ranging from 20 to 60 cm tall. It has a single linear channelled leaf up to 20 cm long and an inflorescence of three to nine flowers, 2 to 5 cm across. Flower colour can vary from white and pink to purple, violet or blue, with the dorsal sepal and petals usually spotted with black. The column is 4 to 5 mm long with apical tufts of white, pink or pale mauve hairs.

The Dotted Sun Orchid is found throughout temperate Australia and New Zealand and also in New Caledonia, growing in grassland and scrub usually in full sun.

Nurseries Selling Hardy Orchids

BRITAIN

Jacques Amand, Clamphill, Stanmore, Middx HA7 3JS
Cypripedium, Calanthe, Pleione, Bletilla, Dactylorhiza

Avon Bulbs, Upper Westwood, Bradford on Avon, Wilts BA15 2AT
Bletilla, Calanthe, Epipactis, Pleione

Blooms of Bressingham Ltd., Bressingham, Diss, Norfolk IP22 2AB
Dactylorhiza species and hybrids

Ian Butterfield, Butterfield's Nursery, Harvest Hill, Bourne End, Bucks SL8 5JJ
Pleione species and hybrids

Paul Christian, Pentre Cottages, Minera, Wrexham, Clwyd, North Wales LL11 3DP
Bletilla, Calanthe, Cypripedium, Dactylorhiza, Goodyera, Pleione

Fortescue Garden Trust, The Garden House, Buckland Monachorum, Devon
Dactylorhiza foliosa

B.D. Goalby, 99 Somerfield Road, Bloxwich, Walsall, West Midlands WS3 2EG
Dactylorhiza foliosa

Holden Clough Nursery, Holden, Bolton-by-Bowland, Clitheroe, Lancs BB7 4PF
Dactylorhiza foliosa, fuchsii, maculata and hybrids

Locking Stumps Pleiones, 7 Eccleston Close, Warrington, Cheshire WA3 7NL
Pleione species, cultivars and hybrids

Paradise Centre, Lamarsh, Bures, Suffolk CO8 5EX
Dactylorhiza species and hybrids

Potterton and Martin, The Cottage Nursery, Moortown Road, Nettleton, Lincs LN7 6HX
Dactylorhiza foliosa

S. Edwards, Westwood Nursery, 65 Yorkland Avenue, Welling, Kent DA16 2LE
Bletilla, Calanthe, Cypripedium, Dactylorhiza, Pleione

Wallace & Barr, The Nurseries, Marden, Kent TN12 9BP
Bletilla, Cypripedium, Habenaria, Pleione

To find out which nurseries stock a particular species, we suggest that you consult *The Plant Finder* devised and compiled by Chris Philip, and edited by Tony Lord, published by Headmain Ltd for the Hardy Plant Society. It appears annually in a new edition.

JAPAN

Japanese Calanthean Society c/o Sanrei Bldg. 4–3 Nihanbashi Muromachi, Chuo-ku, Tokyo

THE UNITED STATES

Orchid Gardens, 6700 Splithand Road, Grand Rapids, Minnesota 55744

We-Du Nurseries, Route #5, Box 724, Marion, NC 28752

Glossary

Acidic: of soils, with a pH of below 7.

Adventitious: buds and roots appearing in abnormal places on the stem of the plant.

Alkaline: of soils, with a pH of above 7.

Anaerobic: without air, sour.

Anther: the portion of a stamen in a flower that produces the pollen.

Apical: at the apex. The tip of a stem.

Aquatic: growing in water.

Asexual: a form of propagation using vegetative parts of plants rather than seed.

Axillary: arising from the axil of leaf and stem.

Backbulb: old pseudobulbs towards the rear of a plant.

Bigeneric: hybrid produced from two genera eg. × Orchiaceras (*Orchis* × *Aceras*).

Bract: leaf-like organ that subtends a flower-stalk.

Breaking: the beginning of growth of a bud.

Callus: (pl. calli): entire or dissected outgrowth on the upper surface of the lip of an orchid flower.

Chlorophyll: green pigment, important in photo-synthesis, found in discrete organelles (chloro-plasts) in the cells of plants, usually in the leaves.

Chlorotic: a yellow appearance in foliage as opposed to the normal healthy green colour.

Clone: a group of plants propagated asexually from one plant.

Deciduous: the habit of shedding leaves, usually for a regular dormant period.

Dormancy: period of non-growth usually asso-ciated with adverse conditions.

Evergreen: retaining leaves throughout the year.

Eye: vegetative bud.

Habitat: the area where a plant grows in its native haunts.

Hardy: frost tolerant.

Humus: decomposing organic matter.

Hyrbid: plant resulting from the crossing of two distinct species.

In vitro: in glass. Refers to the production of plants in glass containers, usually under sterile laboratory conditions.

Inflorescence: the flowers on the floral axis.

Internode: the section of stem between two nodes.

Leafless: growing without leaves.

Lead: the new growth on sympodial orchids.

Lip (also Labellum): the modified odd petal of the orchid flower.

Marginal: of plants, usually refers to those that grow in moist situations close to water.

Medium: the material in which an orchid is grown.

Monopodial: growth habit in which the stem continues to grow indefinitely, rather than forming a resting bud (see sympodial).

Mycorrhiza (pl.mycorrhizae): a fungus inti-mately associated with the root cells of a plant and providing essential nutrients for the growth of the plant.

Node: the point on a stem or pseudobulb where the leaves are attached.

Neutral: of soils, those with a pH of 7.

Offset: lateral shoot, above ground, producing roots, which can be detached and grown on.

Perennial: a plant with a life cycle that continues for more than two years.

Petal: one segment of the corolla, the sterile inner whorl of floral segments, often brightly coloured in orchids.

Pollinium (pl.pollinia): one of the discrete pollen masses in the anther of an orchid.

Procumbent: lying flat. Habit of growth of a stem lying flat on the surface of the medium.

Provenance: the area from which a plant is derived.

Pseudobulb: thickened portion of stem on sympodial orchids.

Pseudobulbous: possessing pseudobulbs.

Rhizome: a horizontal stem, either creeping along the surface or underground.

Rosette: dense spiral of leaves, usually borne at ground level.

Salep: a flour made from ground tubers of certain European and Middle Eastern orchids, claimed to have aphrodisiac properties.

Sepal: one segment of the calyx, the outer sterile whorl of the flower, may be green or coloured in orchids.

Shoot: the new growth of a plant.

Spur: a sack-like to filamentous extension of the base of the lip which may or may not be nectariferous in orchids.

Substance: usually used to refer to the thickness of the floral segments.

Substrate: the material a plant grows in or on.

Succulent: referring to organs of a plant that are fleshy, or to a plant with fleshy organs.

Symbiosis: ecological relationship between members of two different species in which both obtain some benefit from the relationship.

Sympodial: habit of growth in which each shoot has limited growth, new shoots usually arising from the base of older ones.

Terrestrial: growing in the ground.

Tuber: thickened underground stem, applied to the storage organs of orchids, more properly called tuberoids.

Vegetative: parts of a plant not directly involved in flowering: roots, stems and leaves. Form of propagation from same.

Velamen; thick, silvery, protective outer layer that coats the roots of epiphytic and some terrestrial orchids, composed of a layer or layers of dead cells.

Xerophyte: a plant that has morphological adaptations to enable it to survive aridity.

Bibliography

Bailes, C., Clements, M., Cribb, P.J. & **Muir, H.** (1986). *The cultivation of European orchids*, Kew Magazine 3: 8–13.

Bailes, C., Clements, M., Cribb, P.J., Muir, H. & **Tasker, S.** (1987). *The cultivation of European orchids*. Orchid Rev. 95: 19–24.

Baumann, H. & **Künkele, S.** (1982). *Die Wildwachsenden Orchideen Europas*. Kosmos, Stuttgart.

Beckner, J. (1979). *A method of growing the impossible bog orchids*. American Orchid Society Bull. 48: 556–560.

Case, F. W. (1987). *Orchids of the Western Great Lakes*. Cranbrook Inst. Science Bull. 48.

Clements, M. (1982). *Developments in the symbiotic germination of Australian terrestrial orchids*. In Stewart, J. & C. N. van der Merwe eds., Proc. 10th World Orchid Conf. 269–273. South Afr. Orchid Council, Johannesburg.

Clements, M. (1987). *Orchid-fungus: host associations of epiphytic orchids*. Proc. 12th World Orchid Conf.: 80–83.

Clements, M. (1988). *Orchid mycorrhizal associations*. Lindleyana 3: 73–83.

Cribb, P. & **Butterfield, I.** (1988). *The genus Pleione*. Christopher Helm, London.

Darnell, A. W. (1930). *Orchids for the outdoor garden*. Reeve, London.

Dressler, R. *The orchids. Natural history and classification*. Harvard Univ. Press.

Du Puy, D. & **Cribb. P.** (1988). *The genus Cymbidium*. Christopher Helm, London.

Elliot, R. & **Jones, D.** (1982–4). *Encyclopedia of Australian Plants suitable for cultivation*, vols. 2 & 3. Lothian, Melbourne.

Farrer, R. (1908). *My rock garden*. Arnold, London

Grey, C.H. (1938). *Hardy Bulbs*. Williams & Norgate, London.

Heath, R. (1981). *The Collingridge guide to collectors' alpines*. Collingridge, London.

Holman, R. T. (1976). *Cultivation of* Cypripedium calceolus *and* Cypripedium reginae. American Orchid Society Bull. 45: 415–422.

Johnson, M. (1986). *The hardy Chinese orchid* Pleione limprichtii. Kew Mag. 3(2): 73–78.

Kohls, G. (1988). Cypripedium margaritaceum *in Kultur*. Die Orchideen 39(1): 25–26.

Rehder, A. (1940). *Manual of cultivated trees and shrubs*. Macmillan, New York.

Richards, H. (1985). *Cultivation of Australian terrestrial orchids*. Orchid Review 93: 304–306, 323–326 & 359–362.

Richards, H., Wooton, R. & **Datodi, R.** (1988). *Cultivation of Australian native orchids,* ed. 2. Australasian Native Orchid Soc. Victorian Group Inc., Melbourne.

Stewart, J. (1988). *Orchids outside?* The Garden 113: 155–160

Thompson, P. (1977). *Orchids from seed.* H.M.S.O., London.

von Ramin, I. (1976). Erfahrungen in Kultur und Vermehrung von Erdorchideen. Proc. 8th World Orchid Conf.: 364–366.

Warcup, J. (1985). Rhizanthella gardneri *(Orchidaceae), its* Rhizoctonia *endophyte and close association with* Melaleuca uncinata *(Myrtaceae) in Western Australia.* New Phytologist 99: 273–280.

Whitlow, C. E. (1983). Cypripedium *culture in the USA.* Orchid Rev. 91: 300–305.

Index

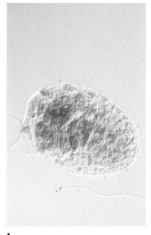

1

2

3

4

1 Embryo of *Pterostylis cucullata* (M. CLEMENTS)

2 Protocorms of *Ophrys apifera* at 4 weeks (A. McROBB)

3 Seedlings of *Ophrys apifera* at 12 weeks (A. McROBB)

4 Seedlings of *Pterostylis fischii* entering dormancy (M. CLEMENTS)

5 Seedlings of *Ophrys apifera* at 14 weeks transferred to compost (A. McROBB)

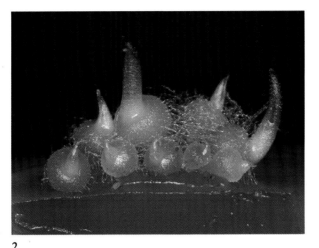

5

6

7

8

9

6 *Aceras anthropophorum*
(C.B.)

7 *Aceras anthrophorum* x
Orchis simia
(J. DELAMAIN)

8 *Amiiostigma keiskei*,
cult. Tokyo (P.C.)

9 *Barlia robertiana*, normal
form (C.B.)

10

10 *Bletilla striata,* cult.Basel (P.C.)

11 *Caladenia dilatata* (P.C.)

12 *Caladenia flava* (P.C.)

12

11

13 *Calanthe discolor*, cult. Tokyo (P.C.)

14 *Calanthe izu-insularis*, cult. Tokyo (C.B.)

15 *Calanthe striata*, cult. Tokyo (P.C.)

15

13

14

16 *Calanthe striata*, cult.Kew (D. MENZIES)

17 *Calanthe tricarinata* (P.C.)

18 *Calanthe tricarinata* x *C.discolor*, cult.Tokyo (P.C.)

18

17

16

19

20

21

22

19 *Calypso bulbosa*, cult.Tokyo (P.C.)

20 *Calypso bulbosa* (C. LUER)

21 *Cephalanthera falcata*, cult.Tokyo (P.C.)

22 *Cephalanthera kurdica* (P.C.)

23 *Corybas orbicularis*, cult.Kew (D. MENZIES)

24 *Chloraea virescens*, cult.Kew (P.C.)

25 *Cremastra appendiculata*, cult.Hiroshima (P.C.)

23

24

25

137

26

27

28

29

26 *Cymbidium goeringii,* cult.Kew (C.B.)

27 *Cymbidium floribundum,* cult.Tokyo (P.C.)

28 *Comperia comperiana,* cult.Kew (R. ZABEAU)

29 *Cypripedium acaule* (C. LUER)

31

30 *C. calceolus* var. *calceolus*, cult.Berne (B. ERNY)

31 *C. calceolus* var. *pubescens* (C.B.)

32 *C. calceolus* var. *parviflorum* (C. GREY-WILSON)

32

33

34

35

33 *C. guttatum* (C. LUER)

34 *C. californicum* (C. LUER)

35 *C. henryi*, cult.Kew (C.B.)

36 *C. japonicum* var. *japonicum*, cult.Tokyo (P.C.)

37 *C. japonicum* var. *formosanum*, cult.Kew (D. MENZIES)

36

37

38 *C. flavum*
   (C. GREY-WILSON)

39 *C. flavum*
   (C. GREY-WILSON)

39

38

40

42

40 *C. margaritaceum*
    (C. GREY-WILSON)
41 *C. montanum* (C. LUER)

41

44

42 *C. reginae*, cult.Geneva (M. KOLAKOWSKI)

43 *C. reginae*, cult.Geneva (M. KOLAKOWSKI)

44 *C. tibeticum* (C. GREY-WILSON)

43

45 *Dactylorhiza elata,* cult.Norfolk (P.C.)

46 *D. elata*, cult.Norfolk (P.C.)

46

48

47 *D. foliosa*, cult.Kew (P.C.)

48 *D. foliosa*, cult.Kew (P.C.)

49 *D. fuchsii* (C. GREY-WILSON)

50 *D. praetermissa*, cult.Kew (P.C.)

51 *D. maculata* var. *transsilvanica*, cult.Geneva (P.C.)

47

49

50

51

52

54

52 *Dactylostalix ringens*, cult.Tokyo (P.C.)

53 *Dendrobium moniliforme*, cult.Hiroshima (P.C.)

54 *Disa uniflora*, cult.Kew (M. SVANDERLIK)

53

55

56

57

55 *Diuris maculata*, cult.Melbourne
    (P.C.)

56 *D. longifolia* (P.C.)

57 *D. punctata*, cult.Melbourne (P.C.)

58 *Epipactis gigantea*, cult.Geneva
    (P.C.)

58

59

60

62

61

59 *E. gigantea*, cult.Geneva (P.C.)

60 *E. palustris*, cult.Kew (M. SVANDERLIK)

61 *Goodyera repens* (P.C.)

62 *G. oblongifolia* (V. SCHWANZ)

63 *Himantoglossum hircinum*, cult.Kew (P.C.)

63

151

64

65

66

67

64 *Ophrys bertolonii*
(P. DAVIES)

65 *O. lutea*, cult.Kew (P.C.)

66 *O. sphegodes*, cult.Kew
(P.C.)

67 *O. tenthredrinifera*,
cult.Kew (P.C.)

68 *O. apifera* on lawn in
Oxfordshire (P.C.)

69 *O. apifera* (P. DAVIES)

68

69

70 *O. vernixia,* cult.Kew
(C.B.)

71 *Orchis italica,* cult.Kew
(P.C.)

72 *O. laxiflora,* cult.Kew
(P.C.)

70

71

72

73

74

73 *O. militaris* (D. TURNER-ETTLINGER)

74 *O. morio*, Norfolk (P.C.)

75

76

78

75 *O. papilionacea*, cult.Kew (P.C.)

76 *O. simia*, cult.Kew (P.C.)

77 *Oreorchis patens*, cult.Hiroshima (P.C.)

78 *Platanthera ciliaris* (C. LUER)

79 *P. grandiflora* (C. LUER)

77

80

82

81

80 *Pleione bulbocodioides*, cult.Bucks
(I. BUTTERFIELD)

81 *P. formosana*, cult.Kew (P.C.)

82 *P. forrestii*, cult.Tokyo (P.C.)

83 *P.* Versailles 'Bucklebury', cult.Kew
(M. ŠVANDERLIK)

83

84

85

84 *P. limprichtii,* cult.Kew
    (M. SVANDERLIK)

85 *P.* Matupi, cult.Bucks
    (I. BUTTERFIELD)

86 *P.* Shantung, cult.Bucks
    (I. BUTTERFIELD)

86

159

87

88

89

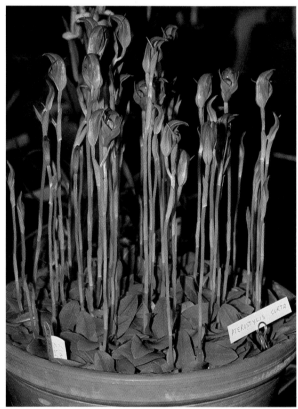

90

91

92

93

87 *Satyrium nepalense*, cult.Kew (C.B.)

88 *Pogonia ophioglossoides* (E. GREENWOOD)

89 *Pterostylis baptistii*, cult.Kew (C.B.)

90 *P. curta*, cult.Dorset (C.B.)

91 *Serapias neglecta*, cult.Kew (P.C.)

92 *S. neglecta* (P.C.)

93 *S. lingua* (P. DAVIES)

94 *Spiranthes spiralis*
   (D. TURNER-ETTLINGER)

94

95 *T. aristata* (P.C.)

96 *T. antennifera* (P.C.)

95

96